Contents

Introduction 6

Chapter 1 7

What And What Not To Eat 7

Chapter 2 11

Early Phase Recovery 11

Early Phase Recipes 12

Bone Broths 12

Chicken Bone Broth 12

Turmeric Ginger Garlic Bone Broth 12

Beef Bone Broth...13

Maitake Garlic Sage Bone Broth 14

Main Dishes/Soups 14

Scrambled Eggs 14

Scrambled Eggs with Cottage Cheese 14

Overnight Oatmeal 15

Baked Salmon in Ginger Orange butter 15

Chicken Vegetable Soup 16

Chicken Turmeric Stew 17

Turkey Tetrazzini..18

Baked Flounder Florentine with Creamy Spinach and Mushroom 18

Baked Halibut in Olive Oil and Herbs 19

Curried Baked Cod 19

White Chicken Chili with Lime and Cauli Rice................20

Creamed Chicken and Mushrooms over Mashed Cauli 21

Butternut Squash Porridge with Apples 21

Egg Salad with Greek Yogurt..23

Curried Chicken Salad with Greek Yogurt.....................23

Tuna Salad with Greek Yogurt 24

Beef Stew...24

Veggie fried Brown Rice with Minced Pork and Shrimp 25

Cream of Broccoli Soup..26

Butternut Squash Bisque 27

Creamy Garlic and Onion Bisque 27

Tuscan White Bean Soup 28

Creamy Potato and Leek soup 28

Loaded Potato Soup...29

Cauliflower Cheese Soup 29

Cream of Mushroom Soup..30

Minestrone 30

Egg Drop Soup 31

Lentil Soup with Kale 32

Carrot Ginger Soup 33

Side Dishes and Smoothies 33

Mashed Cauliflower...33

Cauliflower Rice 34

Creamed Kale..34

Broccoli Casserole...35

Mashed Sweet Potato..35

Baked Apples and Onions 36

Baked Apples and Blueberries 36

Spinach Souffle 36

Mashed Avocado with Lime and Garlic 37

Broccoli Risotto...37

Blueberry Nut Butter Smoothie with Yogurt 38

Banana Berry Smoothie with Yogurt 38

Green Smoothie with Kale, Banana & Avocado...39

Apple Banana Pudding..39

Lemon Garlic Hummus 39

Refried Beans...40

Broccoli Cheese Risotto 40

Cottage Cheese and Mashed Bananas...41

Blueberry Cheesecake Smoothie 41

Chapter 3 44

Long Term Recovery 44

Breakfast: 44

Overnight oats (with 6 variations) 44

Carrot Cake: 44

Tropical Coconut: 45

Strawberry Cheesecake: 45

Apple Cinnamon: 45

Pumpkin Pie: 46

Peach Cobbler 46

Omelets 46

Western: 46

Mexican: 47

3 Cheese: 47

Greek: 47

Frittatas 47

Spinach Bacon Potato Frittata 47

Mushroom, Asparagus and Goat Cheese Frittata....................49

Chicken Breakfast Sausage 50

Sweet Potato Hash 50

Almond Flour Pancakes 51

Additional Sides to eat with breakfast: 52

Snacks to eat any time: 52

Lunch and Dinner Recipes: 53

Grilled Salmon Teriyaki 53

Creamy Lemon Garlic Parmesan Chicken 54

Shrimp Scampi 55

Apple Chicken Burger with Cranberry Sauce 56

Cranberry Sauce...56

Honey Balsamic Chicken 56

Turkey Meatloaf 57

Beef Pot Roast 58

Greek Chicken...59

Asian Glazed Pork Tenderloin 60

Pork Eggroll Stir fry 62

Ginger Lime Halibut 63

Herb Grilled Mahi 63

Ropa Vieja with Brown Rice 64

Salmon Burgers with Guacamole...65

Shrimp Pad Thai with Veggie Noodles 66

Garlic Chicken and Broccoli Casserole 67

Snapper Provençale 68

Artichoke and Asparagus Seafood Gratin 69

Trout Almondine...70

Lamb Burgers with Spinach and Feta..71

Herb Roast Whole Chicken 71

Orange Chicken with Stir fry Veggies..72

Chicken Pineapple Curry..73

Curry Powder 74

Herb Crusted Roast Pork Loin 74

Salisbury Steak with Mushroom Gravy..75

Moo Shu Pork Lettuce Wraps 76

Tom Kha Gai Soup..77

Sides:..78

Creamed Brussels Sprouts 78

Collard Greens 79

Roasted Root Vegetables...79

Cauliflower Mash 80

Roasted Brussels 80

Cauliflower Fried Rice 81

Cilantro Coconut Rice 82

Broccoli Rice 82

Cauliflower Polenta 83

Creamed Spinach 83

Mashed Carrots 84

Glazed Carrots 84

Roasted Butternut Squash 85

Roasted Acorn Squash 85

Zucchini Noodles..85

Butternut Noodles 86

Spaghetti Squash 86

Brown Rice..87

Brown Fried Rice...87

Creamed Swiss Chard 88

Plantain Pilaf 88

Roasted Garlic White Sweet Potato Mash......................................89

Sauteed Garlic Kale 89

Quinoa 89

Lemony Lentil and Quinoa Salad 90

Three Bean Salad 91

Kale Caesar Salad with Crispy Parmesan Chickpeas 92

Sweet & Sour Red Braised Cabbage 94

Homemade Sauerkraut...94

Cabbage Stir fry 95

Parmesan Roasted Broccoli 96

Cauliflower Mac & Cheese..97

Protein and Calorie Table for Key Foods on Your Recovery Diet...................100

In Conclusion 101

Introduction

The world has been swept with a pandemic which is having long term and excruciating effects for those who get infected and survive.

A positive test for COVID-19 can mean many things. So much is still not understood. The virus can leave you completely asymptomatic, kill you, or a million different variations in between.

We don't know why some people get sicker than others, and why some people seem to recover, then months later, develop a new host of symptoms. Then there are the "long-haulers" who survive the initial infection, but stay sick for many months.

The first person I met who contracted COVID-19 is my sister who is a registered nurse. She started with chills and a fever, and quickly progressed to double pneumonia, and almost died. She is still very sick today and her long-term prognosis is unknown at this time. We have no idea why she got so sick, as she had none of the typical "co-morbidities" associated with severe cases of COVID-19.

While I was caring for her, I learned about specific dietary recommendations that her doctors and the medical profession as a whole were making. Since I am a professional chef, specifically in the area of Autoimmune Protocol, I dug into these recommendations and started to formulate a diet plan that would support healing, immunity and muscle building in the aftermath of COVID-19.

I am not a doctor or medical professional of any kind. I am not purporting to cure any disease or affliction. I am definitely not advocating to stop following your doctor's advice, or to stop taking the medications prescribed to you to treat your illness. I am simply taking some basic concepts that anyone can research in depth and applying them to an easy-to-use diet and menu plan to follow as you recover from COVID-19 or any other illness for that matter. It is well known that eating correctly can support the process of healing a great deal.

COVID-19 and other infections cause a massive amount of inflammation in the body. This inflammation manifests in a variety of symptoms, even, in some cases, long after the virus is thought to be eradicated and you have tested negative.

After infection, the resulting "cytokine storm" taking place in the body is what creates all of the inflammation as the body's immune system desperately fights the virus. Frequently, the more severe cases of COVID-19 can result in muscle wasting as the body burns up muscle tissue for energy in the fight to eradicate the virus.

The two most important take-aways from the above summary are inflammation and muscle wasting.

As you begin your journey to full recovery, you want to provide your body with all of the tools it needs to rebuild the lost muscle and reduce the inflammation.

Brain inflammation, which is more commonly referred to as "brain fog" happens quite frequently to sufferers of COVID-19. We will incorporate the following foods into your diet regularly which can help to relieve the brain fog: avocado, blueberries, celery, fatty fish (such as salmon), turmeric curcumin, walnuts, green leafy vegetables, broccoli, cinnamon.

Whether you barely felt sick or are a "long hauler," the dietary recommendations in this book will provide you with the nutritional support you need to bring your body back into balance.

One thing I observed when my sister returned home from the hospital to recover was that everyone wanted to know what they could do to help. They wanted to know if she needed food dropped off or groceries. You can ask a friend to prepare a batch of organic homemade chicken vegetable soup, or a turkey meatloaf with sweet potato mash instead of dropping off fast food from the local pizzeria. The recipes are all here for you to share. People really do want to help. Let them.

Chapter 1

What And What Not To Eat

First, let's start with what **NOT** to eat. These are the most inflammatory foods around, and you need to avoid them during your healing process.

- **Deep fried food of any kind**

- **Fast food**

- **Processed white breads, rolls (refined carbohydrates)**

- Artificial sweeteners

- Cakes, Cookies

- Candy

- Sugars or starches

- Soda

- Chemicals or preservatives

- Vegetable oils other than Olive Oil, Coconut Oil, Avocado Oil, Grass-fed butter

- Alcohol

- Excess sodium

- Salty, preserved nitrate-containing meats, like ham, salami, pepperoni

- Gluten, including white bread, pasta, bread crumbs, croutons (anything with wheat in it)

- Any kind of processed food not listed above

I know this is hard. You are probably not feeling great to begin with, and some takeout would be easy to do, or maybe some frozen meals from the grocery store which you can pop into the microwave. The above list basically precludes doing that.

What should you be eating and drinking:

Basic rule of thumb:

- **To rebuild muscle: 75-100 grams per day of protein (I've broken down how many grams of protein are in meats/fish and eggs in a table at the end of the book).**

- To build up energy levels: Calorie and nutrient dense foods (total 2000-2500 calories per day)

- Stay hydrated: 3 quarts of fluid per day (You'll get that through water, tea, and bone broth)

It's important for everyone to stay hydrated obviously, but when you are recovering from COVID-19 or any other infection, your body is weak, you may have suffered with diarrhea or vomiting, you may be on numerous medications which can dehydrate you and which need fluid to be properly eliminated from the body, or you may be on oxygen or nebulizing treatments which are extremely dehydrating. Anytime you can get some fluids down, please do so.

Another recommendation is to try to eat 6 smaller meals rather than 3 larger ones. It is easier to keep the food down and assimilate it if you don't try to do too much at once. If you are suffering from loss of taste or smell, it is even more challenging to find the will to eat.

<u>**You must eat. Just do it. This is how you are going to get better.**</u>

Nutrient density is important so that you get the most "bang for your buck" in each bite of food you take in. Empty calories are not going to help you get better and are not your friend right now.

Within your 2000-2500 calories per day, after we set aside enough calories for your protein requirements, we need to prioritize your other intake to get the optimal nutrition packed into each day's meals.

The foods you should be eating are:

Protein (100 grams is equal to approximately 400-600 calories):

Wild caught fish, or seafood, avoiding farmed or high mercury fish

Organic Chicken and Turkey

Grass Fed Beef and Lamb

Pastured Pork, sugar free and nitrate free bacon

Organic eggs

Legumes, lentils, peas, beans

Other Foods you should be eating:

Organic Vegetables, with an emphasis on leafy greens, but all vegetables are good

Organic Fruits, with an emphasis on berries and apples, but again all fruits are good

Whole grains, such as oats, brown rice, or quinoa, avoiding gluten-containing grains from wheat which cause inflammation

Nuts and seeds (higher fiber such as almonds and walnuts are better than cashews; pumpkin seeds are very nutritious)

Dairy (grass fed sources) if you can tolerate it and are not suffering with excessive mucus in your illness

Sweet Potatoes

Pink Himalayan Salt or Pure Sea Salt (in moderation) Sea Salt and Pink Himalayan Salt contain trace minerals which can be beneficial to your health.

High quality Fats, including Extra Virgin Olive Oil, Extra Virgin Coconut Oil, Avocados, nut butters, organic grass-fed butter

Bone broths (chicken and beef)

Immune boosting tea which incorporates ginger, lemon and a little organic honey

Anti-Inflammatory Turmeric, Black Pepper and Ginger

Anti-Viral Garlic, Sage, Lemon, raw unfiltered organic apple cider vinegar with the "mother"

You may want to put nightshades on hold for now as they have the tendency to increase inflammation. This would include bell peppers, tomatoes, eggplant and white potatoes. These foods do contain some good nutrients as well, so if you really love them and they have never bothered you in the past, please enjoy in moderation.

Why the need for organic? Organic fruits and vegetables are produced without pesticides which increase inflammation. Grass fed and pastured meats contain much higher levels of macro and micronutrients which contribute to your healing process. Organic poultry and eggs are not given antibiotics and hormones which can also interfere with your healing process. Do the best you can and obtain the highest quality ingredients you can find and/or afford. Be sure to wash all fruits and vegetables thoroughly before cooking.

There are some online companies, such as Butcherbox.com, which can ship great quality meats, poultry and fish directly to your home.

So, you're probably saying right now - this is all well and good, but what the heck should I eat?

This book is broken down into 3 categories:

Early Phase Recovery – if you are one of the unfortunate who was very sick, on oxygen, or maybe even on a ventilator, you may need to stick with softer foods, liquids and purees along with bone broth, to get through the first days. It can be hard to chew or swallow, let alone cut up food, when you are bedridden. Please follow your doctor's recommendations on this.

Long Term Recovery – A collection of delicious nutrient dense breakfast, lunch, dinner and snack recipes to help you on the longer-term road to complete health.

Menu Plans – A suggested week-long menu plan for both Early Phase and Long Term Recovery to help you and your caregiver plan your shopping and cooking.

Chapter 2

Early Phase Recovery

- Drink room temperature water, not iced (aids in digestion)
- Drink soothing decaffeinated tea steeped with Fresh Ginger, Lemon and Organic Honey

- The Early Phase Recovery Recipes and Sample 1 week Menu Plan follow below. All early phase recovery recipes are suitable for long term recovery as well. The nutritional aspects are the same, the main difference is that the early phase diet incorporates mostly soft foods.

Early Phase Recipes

Bone Broths

Chicken Bone Broth

1 large whole organic hormone free chicken

3 stalks of organic celery, washed and rough chopped

3 whole organic carrots, unpeeled, washed and rough chopped

3 whole organic onions, unpeeled and rough chopped

2 bay leaves

2 sprigs organic fresh parsley

1 Tbsp. Sea salt

Place the whole chicken along with any included giblets into the largest stockpot you have. Add the rough chopped vegetables, bay leaves, sea salt and parsley. Fill pot with water, stopping 1" short of the top. Place over a low flame on the back burner and let it simmer all day long. If it comes to a hard boil, reduce heat to lowest flame available so that that your bone broth doesn't all evaporate. Try for 12 hours of simmer time if possible, but at least 6 minimum. Once the broth is cooled, carefully remove and discard the meat, vegetables and bones. Strain the broth into a clean container, cool and refrigerate.

Turmeric Ginger Garlic Bone Broth

1 gallon chicken bone broth

4-6 slices fresh organic ginger root

1 whole head fresh organic garlic, slice top off to expose inner cloves

4-6 slices fresh organic turmeric root (or 1 Tbsp. Dry turmeric powder)

2 sprigs fresh organic parsley

Pour broth into a large stockpot and add other ingredients. Bring to a low simmer and let it go for about 2 hours to infuse. Strain out and discard the aromatics. Store the broth in a clean container under refrigeration.

Beef Bone Broth

4-5 grass fed beef bones, any type (approximately 5 lbs of bones)

3 stalks of organic celery, washed and rough chopped

3 whole organic carrots, unpeeled, washed and rough chopped

3 whole organic onions, unpeeled and rough chopped

3 sprigs organic fresh parsley

1 Tbsp. Sea salt

Preheat oven to 375F. Lay beef bones out in even layer on one tray. Rub lightly with oil. Lay vegetables out in even layer on another tray. Rub lightly with oil. Roast the bones and vegetables in the oven for about 35 minutes until golden brown and fragrant. Let cool then transfer bones and vegetables to your largest stock pot. Add the parsley sprigs and sea salt, then cover with water, stopping 1" from top of the pot. Place over a low flame on the back burner and let it simmer all day long. If it comes to a hard boil, reduce heat to lowest flame available so that that your bone broth doesn't all evaporate. Try for 12 hours of simmer time if possible, but at least 6 minimum. Once the broth is cooled, carefully remove and discard the vegetables and bones and strain the broth into a clean container under refrigeration.

Maitake Garlic Sage Bone Broth

1 gallon beef bone broth

3 oz fresh organic maitake mushrooms (or 1 oz dried)

1 head garlic, top sliced off to expose inner cloves

3 sprigs of fresh sage

Place all ingredients into a stock pot and bring to low simmer. Let it go for 2 hours to infuse flavors. Remove from heat, cool and strain broth into a clean container and store under refrigeration.

Main Dishes/Soups

Scrambled Eggs

Serves 1

2 large organic hormone free eggs

2 tsp. grass-fed butter

1 Tbsp. Milk, any kind

Break eggs into a bowl, add milk, and whisk until frothy. Melt grass-fed butter over low heat in a non-stick sauté pan moving grass-fed butter around to coat pan well. Pour in eggs, and using a wooden spoon stir the eggs frequently until they are cooked through to your preference. Give a light sprinkle of sea salt before serving.

Scrambled Eggs with Cottage Cheese

Add ½ cup of cottage cheese to the eggs while cooking them. This will give an added calorie and protein boost as well as make the eggs very creamy.

Overnight Oatmeal

You may ask why overnight oatmeal instead of cooking it fresh each time? The non-cooking process (which is actually soaking the oats in the refrigerator overnight to soften them) retains more nutrients, is easier to digest, and is a quick convenience.

Per Serving:

½ cup rolled organic oats

1 cup milk, any kind

1 tsp. ground chia or flax seeds

1 Tbsp. Honey or maple syrup

 Place in jar or container with lid. Refrigerate overnight. Enjoy the next morning.

Overnight Oatmeal Variations:

Blueberry Compote, Almond Butter and Cinnamon: ¼ cup organic blueberries cooked in 1 Tbsp. Water and 1 Tbsp. Honey until softened and released juices, 2 Tbsp. Almond butter and dash cinnamon

2 Tbsp. Mashed organic strawberries

2 Tbsp. Nut butter

2 Tbsp. Greek yogurt and honey

2 Tbsp. Pumpkin puree with cinnamon and honey

2 Tbsp. Mashed banana and blueberries

Baked Salmon in Ginger Orange butter
Serves 1

1 6 oz piece wild caught salmon filet, skin and bones carefully removed

1 tsp. orange zest (use a box grater or zester to remove orange zest)

2 Tbsp. Orange juice

½ tsp. fresh ginger root (use box grater to finely grate the ginger)

2 Tbsp. grass-fed butter

Preheat oven to 350F. In small saucepan, melt butter. Add orange juice, orange zest and ginger mixing to combine. Place salmon into a small Pyrex or oven safe dish.   Pour orange ginger butter over the top and bake for 12-16 minutes until fish is cooked through but not dry.

Variations: instead of orange, use lemon zest and juice, or use coconut aminos and scallions for Asian flavor.

Serve with cauliflower rice or sweet potato mash.

Chicken Vegetable Soup

4-6 servings

1 whole chicken organic, hormone free

1 bunch organic celery, washed

1 lb organic carrots

4-5 medium organic yellow onions

3 sprigs organic parsley

2 bay leaves

Sea salt

Get out your large stock pot. Place the whole chicken along with any included giblets into the pot. Cut off the root end of the celery, wash well and add to pot. Cut ends of all the carrots and add to the pot. Cut ends off all the onions and add to the pot. Add bay leaves and parsley. Add water until pot is nearly full leaving an inch or two at the top. Bring to simmer. Let the chicken simmer in there for about an hour. Using tongs, carefully lift the chicken up to expose one of the legs. Test to see if the leg comes off easily. If it does, the chicken is fully cooked. Using a large spoon and pair of tongs, very carefully remove the whole chicken from the simmering water and place it into a bowl to cool. Leave broth simmering in the meantime. After 30-45 minutes, the chicken should be cool enough to handle. Remove the skin and discard. Remove all of the meat and place into a pile, take all of the bones and return them to the pot. You will simmer this for another 2 hours over low heat to extract maximum flavor from the bones. While bones simmer, peel carrots and dice them. Dice up the celery stalks and dice the onions. Place these diced vegetables into a separate bowl. The chicken meat should be diced up as well, carefully picking through to make sure you didn't miss any tiny bones. After the 2 hours of simmering, carefully strain the hot broth through a wire mesh strainer into another large pot if you have one. If not, strain the hot broth into a large bowl. Discard the bones and vegetables, and return hot strained broth the pot. Bring back to simmer and add the diced vegetables. Cook 30 minutes until tender. Add diced chicken meat and remove from heat. Season soup to taste with the sea salt.

Chicken Turmeric Stew

4-6 servings

1 lb boneless skinless organic chicken thighs

1 lb organic carrots, peeled and diced small (2 cups)

1 lb organic celery, diced small (2 cups)

1 lb organic onions, diced small (2 cups)

1 quart organic chicken stock (or bone broth if you have it)

2 Tbsp. Turmeric powder, organic

1 can whole fat organic coconut cream

1 Tbsp. Arrowroot powder or cornstarch for thickening

Whisk together chicken stock, coconut cream and turmeric in a bowl. In a large stockpot, add the chicken thighs, sprinkle all of the diced vegetables over the top and pour the turmeric liquid over all. Cover with a lid and simmer on low for 2 hours. Remove lid and test chicken to see if it is extremely tender. If so, dilute the arrowroot or cornstarch in a little water and add it to the simmering stew until desired thickness is achieved. Season with a little sea salt and very finely chopped cilantro if desired. Stirring of the stew will break of the thighs into fine shreds which are soft and easy to eat.

Serve with mashed sweet potatoes or mashed butternut squash with apples.

Turkey Tetrazzini

4-6 servings

1 lb boneless skinless organic turkey cutlets or tenderloins, diced

1 lb organic carrots, peeled and diced small (2 cups)

1 lb organic celery, diced small (2 cups)

1 lb organic onions, diced small (2 cups)

8 oz organic button mushrooms, diced (2 cups)

1 quart organic chicken stock (or bone broth if you have it)

4 slices sugar free and nitrate free bacon, fried until crisp, drained and chopped very finely

1 can whole fat organic coconut cream

4 Tbsp. Arrowroot powder or cornstarch for thickening

Whisk together chicken stock and coconut cream in a bowl. In a large stockpot, add the diced turkey meat, sprinkle all of the diced vegetables over the top and pour the liquid over all. Cover with a lid and simmer on low for 2 hours. Remove lid and test turkey to see if it is extremely tender. If so, dilute the arrowroot or cornstarch in a little water and add it to the simmering stew until desired thickness is achieved. Stir in fried minced bacon, and season with a little sea salt. Stirring of the stew will break up the turkey into fine shreds which are soft and easy to eat.

Serve with mashed cauliflower.

Baked Flounder Florentine with Creamy Spinach and Mushroom

Serves 1

2 filets (approximately 6 oz) of wild caught flounder or any white flaky fish filets (all skin and bones removed)

1 cup button mushrooms, minced

1 clove garlic minced

2 Tbsp. Minced onions

2 oz fresh or frozen organic spinach, chopped

3 Tbsp. Organic coconut cream or regular heavy cream or full fat Greek Yogurt

Pinch sea salt

2 Tbsp. grass-fed butter

Preheat oven to 350F. Place fish filets in small Pyrex dish. In sauté pan, melt butter, add garlic and mushrooms, and sauté to soften. Add chopped spinach and cream, stir until very creamy. Pour over fish filets and bake for 12-14 minutes until fish is completely cooked through.

Serve with cauliflower rice.

Baked Halibut in Olive Oil and Herbs

Serves 1

1 piece of wild caught Halibut filet (skin and bones removed) approximately 6 oz.

3 Tbsp. Extra virgin olive oil

1 Tbsp. finely minced fresh garlic

2 tsp. finely minced herbs, any type, such as rosemary, dill, oregano, basil

1 Tbsp. fresh lemon juice

Preheat the oven to 350F. Place halibut in small Pyrex dish. Sprinkle garlic and herbs over the fish. Drizzle with olive oil and lemon juice and bake 20-25 minutes until cooked through completely.

Serve with broccoli risotto or spinach souffle.

Curried Baked Cod

Serves 1

1 piece wild caught Cod filet, skin and bones removed, approximately 6 oz.

2 Tbsp. Minced onion

2 tsp. organic curry powder

2 Tbsp. Extra virgin organic coconut oil

½ cup coconut cream or Greek yogurt

Preheat oven to 350F. In a small sauté pan, heat the coconut oil, add the onions and curry powder, until fragrant. Remove from heat and add the coconut cream or yogurt. Place cod in a small Pyrex dish. Spoon curry sauce over the cod filet. Bake 15-18 minutes until fish is cooked completely through.

Serve with roasted root vegetable mash.

White Chicken Chili with Lime and Cauli Rice

3-4 servings

1 lb ground organic hormone free chicken

2 Tbsp. Extra virgin olive oil

1 can white organic cannellini beans

1 large yellow organic onion, peeled and diced

3 cloves organic garlic, minced

2 ripe organic Haas avocados, removed from skin and diced

3 organic scallions, minced

1 green organic zucchini, diced

½ cup fresh lime juice

1 bunch fresh organic cilantro, leaves only, chopped

3 cups organic chicken broth

Sea salt

3 Tbsp. Arrowroot powder or cornstarch, diluted in water

In large sauté pan heat the olive oil, then add the ground chicken meat stirring until cooked through. Add onions, garlic and chicken stock. Simmer until vegetables are tender. Add the beans, lime juice, cilantro, scallions. Taste for seasoning and add sea salt if needed. As the chili simmer, stir in the diluted arrowroot powder to thicken the chili. Fold in the diced avocados at the very end.

Serve with Cauliflower rice or brown rice.

Creamed Chicken and Mushrooms over Mashed Cauli

3-4 servings

1 lb boneless skinless organic hormone free chicken thighs

3 cups organic chicken stock

1 tsp. sea salt

1 tsp. chopped thyme leaves

2 tsp. organic turmeric powder

3 cloves organic garlic, minced

3 oz organic mushrooms, any type, sliced

1 cup full fat Greek Yogurt or organic coconut cream

3 Tbsp. Arrowroot powder or cornstarch, diluted in water

In a large saucepan, put the thighs, chicken stock, turmeric, sea salt, thyme and garlic. Cover and bring to simmer. Simmer on low heat for an hour until the meat is extremely tender. Add the sliced mushrooms and cover again. Cook 5 minutes until mushrooms are tender. Add the yogurt or coconut cream and stir well. Break up the chicken into fine shreds with a spoon. Thicken to taste with arrowroot if desired. Season to taste with more sea salt if needed.

Serve over spaghetti squash or mashed cauliflower.

Butternut Squash Porridge with Apples

2-4 servings

whole butternut squash, peeled, seeds removed and diced into cubes

organic granny smith apples, peeled and diced

Tbsp. grass-fed butter

Tbsp. Organic honey

Pinch of cinnamon

Place the butternut squash into a saucepan and cover with water. Bring to simmer over medium heat and cook until tender. Drain well. Meanwhile, spread the diced apples over a parchment lined tray and bake in the oven at 350 until tender. Remove and cool. Mash the squash well with the butter and honey while it's still hot. Fold in the apples. Sprinkle lightly with cinnamon.

Shepherd's Pie

3-4 servings

3 Tbsp. Extra virgin olive oil

1 lb ground grass fed beef or lamb

3 organic carrots, peeled and diced

3 stalks organic celery, washed and diced

2 organic onions, peeled and diced

1 cup organic frozen peas

2 tsp. fresh minced rosemary

1 organic tomato, diced

2 Tbsp. Minced garlic

2 cups organic beef broth

4 Tbsp. Arrowroot powder or cornstarch, diluted in water.

4 white potatoes, any type, peeled and rough chopped

4 Tbsp. grass-fed butter

4 Tbsp. Greek full fat yogurt

1 cup shredded cheese, any type

In a saucepan, put the potatoes and cover with water. Bring to simmer and cook until tender. While potatoes cook, in a large sauté pan, add the olive oil, then the celery, carrots and onions, stirring until they begin to soften. Add the ground meat and stir around until fully cooked. Add the garlic, tomato and broth, bring to simmer. Add the rosemary and peas and simmer until fully cooked and tender.

Thicken with the diluted arrowroot or cornstarch until creamy. Cool meat mixture completely. Drain the potatoes and mash while hot with the butter and yogurt. Season with sea salt, fold in half the cheese. Pour the cooled meat mixture into a Pyrex or small roasting pan and spread out evenly. Carefully dollop the potato mixture over the top, smoothing it out with a spatula to make an even layer encasing the meat mixture. Sprinkle the remaining cheese over the top. Bake the shepherd's pie in a 350F oven for 35-40 minutes until bubbly and slightly browned on top.

Egg Salad with Greek Yogurt

Serves 1

2 hard-boiled eggs, shells removed

3 Tbsp. Full fat Greek yogurt*

½ tsp. sea salt

½ tsp. onion powder

½ tsp. celery seed

1 tsp. Dijon mustard

Place all ingredients into a small jar and puree using an immersion blender until smooth. This can be made chunky by dicing the eggs and folding the other ingredients in. *I didn't use mayonnaise here because it almost always contains processed vegetable oils and preservatives. If you can find a terrific organic mayonnaise made with extra virgin olive oil, then feel free to substitute that for the yogurt.

Curried Chicken Salad with Greek Yogurt

Serves 1

1 cup cooked organic chicken meat, chopped

1 tsp. organic curry powder

1 tsp. fresh minced ginger

1 tsp. fresh minced cilantro

2 tsp. organic honey

2 Tbsp. Greek yogurt, full fat

Place all ingredients into a small jar and puree using an immersion blender until smooth. This can be made chunky by dicing the chicken and folding the other ingredients in. If you are going chunky style, please consider adding a tablespoon of golden raisins and a sprinkle of chopped nuts. *I didn't use mayonnaise here because it almost always contains processed vegetable oils and preservatives. If you can find a terrific organic mayonnaise made with extra virgin olive oil, then feel free to substitute that for the yogurt.

Tuna Salad with Greek Yogurt

Serves 1

4 oz can line caught mercury free tuna, packed in water

3 Tbsp. Full fat Greek yogurt*

½ tsp. sea salt

½ tsp. onion powder

½ tsp. celery seed

Place all ingredients into a small jar and puree using an immersion blender until smooth. This can be made chunky by flaking the tuna with a fork and folding the other ingredients in. *I didn't use mayonnaise here because it almost always contains processed vegetable oils and preservatives. If you can find a terrific organic mayonnaise made with extra virgin olive oil, then feel free to substitute that for the yogurt.

Beef Stew

4-5 servings

2 lbs. lean grass-fed stew beef, cut into cubes

3 organic carrots, peeled and diced

2 stalks organic celery, washed and diced

1 organic onion, peeled and diced

1 tsp. chopped thyme leaves

1 cup organic green beans, cut into thirds

3 cups organic beef stock

1 organic tomato, diced

3 Tbsp. Organic apple cider vinegar

5 potatoes, any kind, peeled and cubed

2 Tbsp. Extra virgin olive oil

3 Tbsp. Arrowroot or cornstarch diluted in a little water

Heat olive oil in a large pot, season beef with sea salt and add a layer to the bottom and brown it on all sides. This may be done in a few batches. Remove beef to side plate. Add the vegetables to the pot and let them absorb the meat drippings, add the vinegar and the tomatoes, stirring around until liquid evaporates. Then add the browned beef cubes and the stock back to the pot. Cover and simmer on low for 3 hours until it is tender. Add potatoes string beans toward the end of the cooking so they don't get too mushy. When stew is done, stir the diluted arrowroot into the simmering liquid to thicken the gravy. If you are serving this stew chunky you are done. If you need to puree it, then submerge your immersion blender into the stew and puree the stew directly in the pot until smooth.

Veggie fried Brown Rice with Minced Pork and Shrimp

servings

Tbsp. Extra virgin olive oil or avocado oil

organic hormone free eggs, lightly beaten

small organic onion minced

clove organic garlic minced

scallions, minced

2 tsp fresh grated ginger

2 cups brown rice, cooked and cold (don't use fresh hot rice. It will stick and it will be a mess)

2 Tbsp. Gluten free soy sauce or coconut aminos

4 oz ground pastured pork

4 oz wild caught shrimp, peeled, deveined and diced small

Heat a large non-stick sauté pan or wok over high heat add 1 tablespoon of oil. Add eggs and scramble. When cooked, remove and set aside. Add a bit more oil. Add onion, scallion, ginger and garlic, stir until fragrant. Add the raw diced shrimp and pork. Stir constantly until fully cooked through. Add the rice, then the soy sauce. Stir well, then return egg to the rice and stir to combine. Season with additional soy sauce or sea salt if needed.

Cream of Broccoli Soup

3-4 servings

1 large head of organic broccoli, leaves removed, tough outer skin on stem removed and chopped

2 medium organic onions, peeled and chopped

2 medium organic carrots, peeled and chopped

1 can organic coconut cream

4 Tbsp. extra virgin organic coconut oil

1 quart organic chicken stock

Heat oil in large soup pot, add onions and carrots and stir around for a bit to soften. Add the chopped broccoli and then the chicken stock. Cover pot and bring to low boil. Cook for about 30 minutes until broccoli is extremely tender. Add the coconut cream and a little sea salt. Use an immersion blender to puree soup directly in pot until it is smooth. Be careful soup doesn't splatter your arm. Serve with some finely grated cheddar cheese stirred in if desired.

Butternut Squash Bisque

3-4 servings

1 large organic butternut squash, peeled, seeded and chopped into cubes

2 medium organic onions, peeled and chopped

2 medium organic carrots, peeled and chopped

1 can organic coconut cream

4 Tbsp. extra virgin organic coconut oil

1 quart organic chicken stock

Heat oil in large soup pot, add onions and carrots and stir around for a bit to soften. Add the chopped squash and then the chicken stock. Cover pot and bring to low boil. Cook for about 30 minutes until squash is extremely tender. Add the coconut cream and a little sea salt. Use an immersion blender to puree soup directly in pot until it is smooth. Be careful soup doesn't splatter your arm. Serve with a dusting of fresh nutmeg or cinnamon if desired.

Creamy Garlic and Onion Bisque

3-4 servings

6 medium organic onions, peeled and chopped

1 cup peeled organic garlic cloves (most stores have these available peeled and ready to go)

1 can organic coconut cream

4 Tbsp. extra virgin olive oil

1 quart organic chicken stock

Heat oil in large soup pot, add onions and garlic and 1-quart stir over low heat until they begin to caramelize. Add the chicken stock. Cover pot and bring to low boil. Cook for about 30 minutes until vegetables are extremely tender. Add the coconut cream and a little sea salt. Use an immersion blender to puree soup directly in pot until it is smooth. Be careful soup doesn't splatter your arm. Serve with some finely grated cheddar or parmesan cheese stirred in if desired.

Tuscan White Bean Soup

3-4 servings

2 cans organic cannellini beans (white kidney) drained and rinsed

3 cloves garlic minced

1 medium potato, peeled and cubed

1 tsp. fresh thyme leaves, chopped

3 cups organic chicken stock

2 Tbsp. Extra virgin olive oil

In large saucepan, heat the olive oil, add the garlic and potato and sauté until they begin to caramelize, add a little water if necessary to cook potatoes through. Add the drained beans and the thyme along with the broth. Bring to a simmer. Use an immersion blender to puree the soup directly in the pot. To desired consistency. Serve topped with extra virgin olive oil.

Creamy Potato and Leek soup

3-4 servings

3 white organic sweet potatoes or regular russet potatoes if you prefer

4 whole organic leeks

½ cup extra virgin olive oil

1 quart organic chicken stock

1 cup Greek yogurt

4 Tbsp. Fresh chives

Wash the leeks well to remove any sand, cut into slices. Peel and chop the potatoes. Heat the olive oil in a large saucepan and sweat the leeks until they wilt. Add the potatoes and broth. Bring to simmer. When potatoes are tender, add the yogurt and puree directly in the pot until smooth using an immersion blender. Season to taste with sea salt. Garnish with fresh chives.

Loaded Potato Soup

3-4 servings

4 large organic potatoes, sweet or regular, peeled and chopped

1 quart organic chicken stock

1 can organic coconut cream

1 organic onion, peeled and diced

3 Tbsp. Extra virgin olive oil

4 slices sugar and nitrate free bacon, cooked until crisp and chopped finely

4 organic scallions, minced

1 cup shredded cheddar cheese

Sea salt

In a large saucepan, heat the olive oil, add the onions and sweat for a few minutes. Add the potatoes, and add the stock. Bring to simmer. Cook until potatoes are tender. Add coconut cream and puree with immersion blender directly in pot until very smooth. Season to taste with sea salt. Add the finely minced bacon and scallions, sprinkle with cheddar.

Cauliflower Cheese Soup

-4 servings

large head organic cauliflower

large yellow organic onion

qt. organic chicken stock

large potato, any type

1 cup shredded cheddar cheese

1 cup whole milk coconut cream or Greek yogurt, full fat

Sea salt

Remove core and leaves of cauliflower and rough chop. Add to a large saucepan. Peel and rough chop the potato, peel and rough chop the onion and add all of them to the pot. Add the chicken stock and bring to low boil. Lower heat, and simmer until all of the vegetables are extremely tender, approximately 20 minutes. Use an immersion blender to puree the soup directly in the pot. Add the coconut cream or yogurt and the cheddar cheese. Stir to combine. Season to taste with the sea salt.

Cream of Mushroom Soup

3-4 servings

2 lbs. fresh organic mushrooms, any type

2 organic yellow onions

4 cloves organic garlic, minced

4 Tbsp. Extra virgin olive oil

4 cups organic beef or vegetable broth

2 tsp. chopped thyme leaves

1 tsp. sea salt

1 cup full fat Greek yogurt or coconut cream

Heat the oil in a large saucepan, add onions, garlic and mushrooms and stir for a few minutes until they soften. Add the broth, thyme and sea salt. Bring to simmer and cook until all vegetables are tender, approximately 20 minutes. Use an immersion blender to puree the soup directly in the pot until smooth. Stir in 1 cup of coconut cream or full fat Greek yogurt. Season to taste with the sea salt.

Minestrone

4 servings

3 organic carrots, peeled and diced

2 organic yellow onions, peeled and diced

3 stalks organic celery, washed and diced

1 organic zucchini, washed and diced

1 can organic red kidney beans, drained and rinsed

½ lb organic string beans, washed and cut into thirds

4 cloves organic garlic, minced

1 large organic tomato, diced or 1 can of organic diced tomatoes

1 tsp. minced thyme

1 tsp. minced rosemary

1 tsp. dry oregano

2 tsp. sea salt

4 cups organic chicken stock

In a large pot, put the celery, carrots, onions, garlic, string beans, tomato, herbs and chicken stock. Bring to simmer. Cook over low heat until vegetables are tender. Add zucchini and beans and bring back to simmer to lightly cook zucchini for a few minutes. Season with sea salt as needed.

Egg Drop Soup

2-3 servings

1 qt. organic chicken broth (save a little to dilute the cornstarch)

½ tsp. fresh minced ginger

2 tsp. coconut aminos or gluten free soy sauce

1 tsp. toasted sesame oil

3 organic hormone free eggs, beaten

¼ cup scallions, finely minced

1 ½ Tbsp. Cornstarch, diluted in a little cup of the cold chicken stock

½ tsp. sea salt

¼ tsp. ground pepper (if you can tolerate spices, otherwise omit)

In a saucepan, place the chicken broth, ginger, coconut aminos, sesame oil, sea salt and pepper (if using), over medium heat, bring to a simmer. While it is simmering, slowing whisk in the cornstarch mixture. Cook for a minute, then use a spoon to slowly stir the soup in a circular motion, and stream the eggs in at the same time, to create the ribbons. Stir in the minced scallions and cook one more minute.

Lentil Soup with Kale

4 servings

2 Tbsp. Extra virgin olive oil

1 organic onion, finely chopped

2 organic carrots, peeled and finely chopped

2 organic celery stalks, washed and finely minced

1 Tbsp. organic garlic minced

1 cup brown or green lentils

2 tsp. dry Italian seasoning

2 bay leaves

1 can organic diced tomatoes

4 cups organic chicken or vegetable broth

2 cups finely chopped organic kale

½ tsp. sea salt

Rinse lentils and set aside. Heat oil in a large pot, add the onion, garlic, celery, and carrot. Sauté 2 minutes until aromatic. Add lentils and stock, Italian seasoning and sea salt. Bring to boil, reduce heat and simmer covered 15 minutes. At this point, add the tomatoes and kale. Simmer another 15 minutes until lentils are completely tender. Use your ladle to mash some of the lentils in the pot. This will thicken the soup. Or you can use your immersion blender and pulse it a few times directly in the pot to puree the soup.

Carrot Ginger Soup

4 servings

12 large organic carrots, peeled and chopped

2 Tbsp. Extra virgin coconut oil

1 large organic onion, peeled and diced

3 cloves of garlic minced

2 tablespoons fresh organic ginger, grated on box grater

1 tsp. sea salt

4 cups organic chicken stock

1 cup organic coconut cream or Greek yogurt full fat

In a large pot, heat the coconut oil. Add the carrots, onions and garlic and cook until onions become a bit soft. Add grated ginger and salt then pour in the stock just enough to cover the vegetables. Simmer over medium low heat until carrots are extremely tender. Puree soup directly in the pot with the immersion blender, then stir in the coconut cream or yogurt.

Side Dishes and Smoothies

Mashed Cauliflower

2-3 Servings

1 head organic cauliflower

2 Tbsp. grass-fed butter, extra virgin olive oil or extra virgin coconut oil

1 tsp. sea salt

Trim leaves and stem from cauliflower, wash well and rough chop. Place in a saucepan and cover with water. Simmer until tender, drain very well. Add the butter or oil and sea salt and puree with an immersion blender or a food processor until smooth.

Cauliflower Rice

2-3 Servings

1 head organic cauliflower

1 small yellow onion

2 Tbsp. Extra virgin olive oil

Sea salt

Trim leaves and stem from cauliflower and break into florets. Put florets one handful at a time into the bowl of a food processor and pulse a few times until rice sized pieces are formed. Scrape each batch into a bowl until it is all processed. Mince the onion very finely. In a large non-stick sauté pan, heat the olive oil, add the onion and sweat until soft, add the cauliflower rice and stir frequently. Add a few tablespoons of water then cover to let the rice steam for 2 minutes. Remove cover stir and then season to taste with sea salt.

Creamed Kale

3-4 Servings

1 bunch organic kale

1 cup coconut cream or heavy cream

1 small organic yellow onion, minced

2 Tbsp. Extra virgin olive oil

2 cloves garlic, minced

1 tsp. sea salt

Wash kale well, remove leaves from stems and chop finely. Heat the olive oil in a large sauté pan, add the onion and garlic and sauté until softened. Add kale leaves and stir until wilted. Add the coconut or heavy cream. Bring to a simmer. Simmer until thickened and kale is tender. Season to taste with sea salt.

Broccoli Casserole

4-5 Servings

2 bunches organic broccoli

2 small yellow onions, minced

3 garlic cloves minced

3 Tbsp. Extra virgin olive oil

1 cup coconut or heavy cream

1 cup grated cheese, any kind

1 tsp. sea salt

Remove leaves and tough stems from broccoli and rough chop. Place into a saucepan and cover with water. Bring to simmer and simmer until crisp tender. Drain well. In a large sauté pan, heat the olive oil and sauté the onion and garlic until softened. Add the cream and bring to a simmer. Add the broccoli and the cheese and stir to combine. Pour into a Pyrex baking dish and bake at 350F for 35 minutes until bubbly.

Mashed Sweet Potato

3-4 Servings

3 organic sweet potatoes, orange or white

3 Tbsp. grass-fed butter

3 Tbsp. organic honey (optional)

1 tsp. sea salt

1 cup coconut or heavy cream or Greek yogurt

Peel and rough chop the potatoes, place into a saucepan and cover with water. Bring to a simmer and cook until tender. Drain well, add the butter, cream, honey (if using), and sea salt. Mash well using a hand potato masher.

Baked Apples and Onions

3-4 Servings

4 organic apples, any type, peeled, cored and cut into quarters

2 small yellow organic onions, sliced

Pinch sea salt

Preheat oven to 350F. Toss apples and onions together and sprinkle with salt, place into small Pyrex, cover and bake 35 minutes or until tender.

Baked Apples and Blueberries

3-4 Servings

4 organic apples, any type, peeled, cored and cut into quarters

½ cup organic blueberries

Preheat oven to 350F. Toss apples and blueberries together, place into small Pyrex, cover and bake 35 minutes or until tender.

Spinach Souffle

3-4 Servings

1 bag washed organic baby spinach, 12 oz.

1 cup heavy cream or coconut cream

1 small yellow organic onion, minced

2 cloves organic garlic, minced

2 Tbsp. Extra virgin olive oil

2 Tbsp. Cornstarch or arrowroot powder

2 organic hormone free eggs

Pinch mace powder (optional)

Preheat oven to 375F. Chop the spinach. Heat the olive oil in a large nonstick pan, sauté the onion and garlic until softened. Add the spinach and cook for 1 minute just to wilt. Remove and drain well. Cool completely. Whisk together cream, eggs, cornstarch, mace (if using) and sea salt. Fold spinach into this mixture, and pour into a small Pyrex. Put dish uncovered into oven and bake until puffed up and lightly browned, approximately 35 minutes.

Mashed Avocado with Lime and Garlic

1 Serving

1 ripe organic Haas avocado

1 clove organic garlic minced

1 organic lime, juice only (2 Tbsp.)

Pinch sea salt

Remove flesh of avocado from skin, add other ingredients and mash with fork.

Broccoli Risotto

2-4 Servings

head organic broccoli

small yellow onion, minced

cloves organic garlic, minced

Tbsp. Extra virgin olive oil

ripe organic Haas avocados

organic lime, juice only

Tbsp. Greek yogurt, or coconut cream

1 tsp. sea salt

2 Tbsp. Fresh cilantro, finely chopped

Remove leaves and tough stems from broccoli. Break into florets and put into bowl of food processor. Pulse to form small pieces of broccoli "rice." Remove rice to bowl. Heat olive oil in a nonstick sauté pan. Add the onions and garlic. Add the broccoli rice, stir to coat. Add a few tablespoons of water then cover broccoli rice to steam for 2 minutes. Uncover, stir and remove from heat. In a bowl, mash the avocado, lime juice, yogurt, sea salt and cilantro together until very smooth. Fold into the broccoli rice. Serve warm.

Blueberry Nut Butter Smoothie with Yogurt

Serves 1

1 cup fresh or frozen organic blueberries

2 tablespoons organic nut grass-fed butter, any kind

1 cup Greek yogurt

2 tablespoons raw honey

1/4 cup nut milk or regular milk

Put all ingredients into a blender and blend on high until smooth.

Banana Berry Smoothie with Yogurt

Serves 1

1 organic banana peeled

1 cup berries, organic, any kind

1 cup Greek yogurt

¼ cup milk, any kind

Put all ingredients into a blender and blend on high until smooth.

Green Smoothie with Kale, Banana & Avocado

Serves 1

1 cup organic kale leaves, washed and finely chopped

1 small organic banana

1 small organic avocado

1 cup organic unsweetened apple juice

Put all ingredients into a blender and blend on high until smooth.

Apple Banana Pudding

Serves 2

3 organic apples, any kind, peeled and cored

3 organic bananas, peeled and chopped

Pinch cinnamon (optional)

Chop apples and place in steamer basket. Steam until tender. Add apples and bananas to a food processor or blender and puree until smooth. Add cinnamon if desired.

Lemon Garlic Hummus

2-3 Servings

1 can organic garbanzo beans

1 organic lemon, juice only

2 cloves organic garlic, minced

3 Tbsp. Extra virgin olive oil

2 Tbsp. Organic Tahini paste

1 tsp. sea salt

Drain beans and rinse. Add all of the ingredients to a food processor and puree until smooth.

Refried Beans

1 can organic pinto, pink or black beans

2 tsp. granulated garlic

3 Tbsp. Extra virgin olive oil

2 tsp. sea salt

½ cup grated cheddar cheese

Preheat oven to 350F. Drain beans well. Add to bowl of food processor with garlic, olive oil and sea salt. Puree until smooth. Spread into a small Pyrex dish, sprinkle with cheese and bake 15 minutes until bubbly.

Broccoli Cheese Risotto

Serves 3-4

2 cups brown rice, cooked and cooled

1 cup coconut cream or heavy cream

1 cup grated sharp cheddar cheese

2 cloves organic garlic, minced

1 small organic yellow onion, minced

2 Tbsp. Extra virgin olive oil

2 cups organic broccoli, leaves and stems removed, cut into small bite sized florets

1 tsp. sea salt

Put florets into a small saucepan and cover with water. Simmer for 5 minutes until just tender. Drain. Heat olive oil in large nonstick sauté pan. Add onion, garlic and rice. Stir until onion softened. Add cream, sea salt and broccoli. Stir until bubbly, add cheese, stir until melted and serve.

Cottage Cheese and Mashed Bananas

Serves 1

½ cup full fat cottage cheese

1 organic banana

Mash banana with fork, fold into cottage cheese. Serve.

Blueberry Cheesecake Smoothie

Serves 1

1 cup organic fresh or frozen blueberries

1 cup full fat cottage cheese

½ cup milk, any kind

1 organic banana

¼ tsp. cinnamon

Put all ingredients into a blender and blend on high until smooth.

~~~~~~

Below is a week-long suggested meal plan for your Early Phase Recovery. If you like eggs for breakfast every day, by all means have them. This is only meant to be a guideline. Try to drink some bone broth every day. It is excellent for your gut health, which is the center of your immune system. Try to get some turmeric into your diet as often as possible. Sprinkle it into your soups, smoothies, eggs, stews etc. Turmeric is an important anti-inflammatory spice. Fresh ginger is great for your immune system and to soothe digestion, so is recommended to incorporate some each day. All of the menu items are meant to be nutrient dense, caloric, high in protein and easy to eat when you are in early stage of recovery from illness. This suggested meal plan provides approximately 2000-2500 calories per day with at least 75 grams of protein. There is a calorie/protein breakdown chart at the end of this book to help guide you when planning your own menu.

EARLY PHASE RECOVERY SAMPLE ONE WEEK MEAL PLAN

	SUNDAY	MONDAY	TUESDAY	WEDNESDAY	THURSDAY	FRIDAY	SATURDAY
MEAL 1 **BREAKFAST**	2 SCRAMBLED EGGS IN GRASS-FED BUTTER, HALF SLICED AVOCADO, ½ CUP FULL FAT COTTAGE CHEESE WITH BANANAS LEMON GINGER TEA WITH HONEY	OVERNIGHT OATS (2 CUPS) WITH ALMOND BUTTER (2 TBL), BLUEBERRIES, AND CINNAMON LEMON GINGER TEA WITH HONEY	2 EGGS SCRAMBLED IN GRASS-FED BUTTER WITH HALF SLICED AVOCADO, QUINOA WITH ONIONS (1 CUP) LEMON GINGER TEA WITH HONEY	OVERNIGHT OATS, MASHED BANANA, BAKED APPLE, CINNAMON LEMON GINGER TEA WITH HONEY	2 EGGS SCRAMBLED WITH COTTAGE CHEESE, BROWN RICE (1 CUP), BANANA SLICES WITH 2 TBL. NUT BUTTER LEMON GINGER TEA WITH HONEY	OVERNIGHT OATS, CARROT CAKE LEMON GINGER TEA WITH HONEY	2 EGGS SCRAMBLED, ONION QUINOA, SLICED AVOCADO LEMON GINGER TEA WITH HONEY
MEAL 2 **SNACK**	BONE BROTH (ANY KIND) 2 CUPS	GREEN SMOOTHIE WITH KALE, BANANA, AVOCADO AND UNSWEETENED ORGANIC APPLE JUICE, 2 CUPS	BONE BROTH (ANY KIND) 2 CUPS	EGG SALAD WITH GREEK YOGURT, TENDER LETTUCE, AVOCADO DRIZZLED WITH 2 TBL. EXTRA VIRGIN OLIVE OIL	BONE BROTH (ANY KIND) 2 CUPS	LEMON GARLIC HUMMUS WITH PEELED SLICED CUCUMBER	BONE BROTH (ANY KIND) 2 CUPS
MEAL 3 **LUNCH**	PUREE OF BEEF STEW 2 CUPS	CURRIED CHICKEN SALAD 8 OZ WITH 2 OZ GREEK YOGURT (1 CUP), TENDER LETTUCE, PEELED SLICED APPLE	PUREE BEEF STEW, 2 CUPS	TURMERIC CHICKEN STEW, 2 CUPS	TUNA SALAD WITH GREEK YOGURT, TENDER LETTUCE, AVOCADO SLICES	SHEPHERD'S PIE, 2 CUPS	CHICKEN VEGETABLE SOUP, 2 CUPS
MEAL 4 **SNACK**	BAKED APPLES AND BLUEBERRY 1 CUP LEMON	BUTTERNUT SQUASH BISQUE, 2 CUPS LEMON GINGER TEA	BLUEBERRY CHEESECAKE SMOOTHIE LEMON GINGER	APPLE BANANA PUDDING LEMON GINGER TEA	BANANA BERRY SMOOTHIE WITH YOGURT LEMON	SCOOP OF COTTAGE CHEESE WITH SLICED BANANAS	BLUEBERRY NUT BUTTER SMOOTHIE WITH YOGURT LEMON

	GINGER TEA WITH HONEY	WITH HONEY	TEA WITH HONEY	WITH HONEY	GINGER TEA WITH HONEY	LEMON GINGER TEA WITH HONEY	GINGER TEA WITH HONEY
MEAL 5 **DINNER**	TURMERIC CHICKEN STEW, 2 CUPS	SHEPHERD'S PIE, 2 CUPS	BAKED SALMON 6 OZ WITH BROCCOLI RISOTTO	CHICKEN VEGETABLE SOUP, 2 CUPS	PUREE OF BEEF STEW, 2 CUPS	TURMERIC CHICKEN STEW, 2 CUPS	BAKED HALIBUT IN OLIVE OIL AND HERBS WITH CREAMED KALE
MEAL 6 **SNACK**	LEMON GARLIC HUMMUS ½ CUP WITH PEELED SLICED CUCUMBER LEMON GINGER TEA WITH HONEY	BONE BROTH (ANY KIND) 2 CUPS LEMON GINGER TEA WITH HONEY	CHICKEN VEGETABLE SOUP, 2 CUPS LEMON GINGER TEA WITH HONEY	BONE BROTH (ANY KIND) 2 CUPS LEMON GINGER TEA WITH HONEY	BUTTERNUT SQUASH BISQUE LEMON GINGER TEA WITH HONEY	BONE BROTH (ANY KIND) 2 CUPS LEMON GINGER TEA WITH HONEY	APPLE BANANA PUDDING LEMON GINGER TEA WITH HONEY

The easiest way to handle menu planning and cooking when you are doing it all at home is to make a larger batch of each item so that it can be used throughout the week. Anything you won't be eating that week can be portioned out and frozen for next week.

For the above sample menu, you will be serving overnight oats 3 times, so you will need 6 cups for the week. Bone broth is 2 cups per day, so make one big pot and utilize it all week long. Turmeric chicken stew shows up 3 times, beef stew shows up twice, shepherd's pie shows up twice, hummus shows up twice, chicken vegetable soup three times, butternut bisque twice, then everything else is very quick and easy, such as baked fish, chicken salad, egg salad, baked apples, scrambled eggs, and smoothies. All of those meals take less than 10 minutes to prepare.

The item that takes the longest to prepare is the bone broth. It is important to drink bone broth each day because of the protein and vital collagen it contains. It needs to simmer in a large pot about 12 hours to extract all of the nutrients from the bones. Another option is to purchase some decent quality bone broth at your local organic foods market, but it is quite expensive. A final option is to purchase vital collagen powder from grass fed sources and add it to your food.

Chapter 3

Long Term Recovery

During this phase, we are assuming that you are able to sit up and eat. That you are able to cut solid food, chew and swallow easily. This opens up a lot more food options to you, and we will continue with the same calorie and protein goals as before. Just because you are starting to feel better doesn't mean it's time to start eating processed food devoid of nutrients.

Breakfast:

Overnight oats (with 6 variations)

You may ask why overnight oatmeal instead of cooking it fresh each time? The non-cooking process (which is actually soaking the oats in the refrigerator overnight to soften them) retains more nutrients, is easier to digest, and is a quick convenience.

Per Serving:

½ cup rolled organic oats

1 cup milk, any kind

1 tsp. ground chia or flax seeds

1 Tbsp. Honey or maple syrup

Place in jar or container with lid. Refrigerate overnight. Enjoy the next morning either hot or cold.

Variations:

Carrot Cake:

1/2 teaspoon vanilla extract
2 tablespoons honey or maple syrup

1 large carrot, peeled and shredded

2 tablespoons softened cream cheese

1/4 cup raisins

1/2 teaspoon ground cinnamon

Tropical Coconut:

1/2 teaspoon vanilla extract

2 tablespoons honey or syrup

1/3 cup chopped fresh or canned pineapple

1/3 cup chopped ripe mango

1/2 ripe banana, chopped or mashed

Tbsp. unsweetened flaked coconut

Strawberry Cheesecake:

1/2 teaspoon vanilla extract

tablespoons honey or maple syrup

1/4 cup chopped fresh strawberries

tablespoons softened cream cheese

zest and juice of 1/2 lemon

Apple Cinnamon:

cup peeled diced organic apple, any kind

tsp. cinnamon

8 tsp. nutmeg

tablespoons honey or maple syrup

tablespoons toasted chopped walnuts

Pumpkin Pie:

¼ cup part-skim ricotta cheese

2 tablespoons pumpkin puree

1 tablespoon pure maple syrup

¼ teaspoon vanilla extract

⅛ teaspoon ground nutmeg

Peach Cobbler

½ teaspoon vanilla extract

2 tablespoons pecans coarsely chopped

1 cup fresh or frozen organic peeled peaches, finely diced

2 tablespoons honey

1/8 tsp. cinnamon

⅛ tsp. nutmeg

Omelets

2-3 organic hormone free eggs whisked

1 Tbsp. Milk, any kind

¼ tsp sea salt

2 Tbsp. Grass-fed butter or extra virgin olive oil

Variations:

Western:

2 Tbsp. Each of diced onions, diced bell peppers, diced sugar and nitrate free ham and ¼ cup of shredded cheese

Mexican:

2 Tbsp. Each of diced onions, diced tomatoes, diced avocados, ¼ cup shredded Mexican cheese, 1 Tbsp. Chopped cilantro

3 Cheese:

3 Tbsp. Each of any 3: cheddar, gouda, swiss, mozzarella, brie, goat, feta, muenster, (avoid American, it is processed with lots of food coloring) Add a sprinkle of fresh chopped herbs

Greek:

2 Tbsp. Each of diced onions, diced tomatoes, ¼ cup crumbled feta cheese, sprinkle of fresh or dry oregano.

Heat the butter in a nonstick sauté pan over medium heat. Whisk eggs, with milk and salt and pour into the pan. Using a wooden spoon, pull back the edges of the omelet allowing the liquid to fill in the edges and cook. Turn down heat to low, sprinkle all the omelet toppings over the omelet evenly and cover for 2-3 minutes until top of omelet is set and cheese if using is melted. Gently fold the omelet onto a serving plate.

Frittatas

Your basic ratio for a frittata is as follows:

For every six eggs, use 1/4 cup heavy cream or coconut cream, 1 cup cheese, and 2 cups total of vegetables and/or meat. Use a cast iron or oven-safe non-stick skillet to bake the frittata.

Variations:

Spinach Bacon Potato Frittata

4-6 Servings

6 large organic hormone free eggs, enough to cover the ingredients

1/4 cup heavy cream or coconut cream

1 teaspoon sea salt, divided

4 slices thick-cut sugar and nitrate free bacon (8 ounces), chopped

2 small organic sweet potatoes, peeled and thinly sliced

1/4 teaspoon freshly ground black pepper

2 cups organic baby spinach (2 ounces)

2 cloves organic garlic, minced

2 teaspoons fresh thyme leaves

1 cup shredded cheese, such as Gruyere, Fontina, or cheddar

Arrange a rack in the middle of the oven and heat to 400°F.

Whisk the eggs, heavy cream, and 1/2 teaspoon salt together in a small bowl; set aside.

Cook the bacon. Place the bacon in a cold 10- to 12-inch nonstick oven-safe frying pan or cast-iron skillet, then turn the heat to medium-high. Cook the bacon, stirring occasionally, until crisp, 8 to 10 minutes. Remove the bacon with a slotted spoon to a paper towel-lined plate and pour off all but 2 tablespoons of the fat. (If omitting the bacon, heat 2 tablespoons oil in the skillet, then proceed with adding the potatoes).

Sauté the potatoes in bacon fat. Return the pan to medium-heat, add the potatoes and sprinkle with the pepper and the remaining 1/2 teaspoon salt. Cook, stirring occasionally, until tender and lightly browned, 4 to 6 minutes.

Wilt the spinach with the garlic and thyme. Pile the spinach into the pan with the garlic and thyme, and cook, stirring, for 30 seconds to 1 minute or until spinach wilts. Add the bacon back to the pan and stir to evenly distribute.

Add the cheese. Spread the vegetables into an even layer, flattening with a spatula. Sprinkle the cheese on top and let it just start to melt.

Pour the egg mixture into the skillet. Pour the egg mixture over the vegetables and cheese. Tilt the pan to make sure the eggs settle evenly over all the vegetables. Cook for a minute or two until you see the eggs at the edges of the pan beginning to set.

Bake the frittata for 8 to 10 minutes. Bake until the eggs are set, 8 to 10 minutes. To check, cut a small slit in the center of the frittata. If raw eggs run into the cut, bake for another few minutes; if the eggs are set, pull the frittata from the oven.

For a browned, crispy top, run the frittata under the broiler for a minute or two at the end of cooking.

Cool and serve. Cool in the pan for 5 minutes, then slice into wedges and serve.

Mushroom, Asparagus and Goat Cheese Frittata

4-6 Servings

6 large eggs, enough to cover the ingredients

1/4 cup heavy cream or coconut cream

1 teaspoon sea salt, divided

2 tablespoon grass-fed butter

1 cup organic mushrooms, any type, sliced

1 bunch organic asparagus spears, trimmed and cut into 1/2-inch pieces

4 tablespoons chopped green onion

5 oz. goat cheese

Arrange a rack in the middle of the oven and heat to 400°F.

Whisk the eggs, heavy cream, and 1/2 teaspoon salt together in a small bowl; set aside.

Melt butter in a 10- to 12-inch nonstick oven-safe frying pan or cast-iron skillet.

Sauté the mushrooms and asparagus until tender. Add the remaining 1/2 teaspoon sea salt.

Distribute evenly over the bottom of the pan.

Spread the vegetables into an even layer, flattening with a spatula. Sprinkle the cheese on top and let it just start to melt.

Pour the egg mixture over the vegetables and cheese. Tilt the pan to make sure the eggs settle evenly over all the vegetables. Sprinkle with the green onions. Cook for a minute or two until you see the eggs at the edges of the pan beginning to set.

Bake the frittata for 8 to 10 minutes. Bake until the eggs are set, 8 to 10 minutes. To check, cut a small slit in the center of the frittata. If raw eggs run into the cut, bake for another few minutes; if the eggs are set, pull the frittata from the oven. For a browned, crispy top, run the frittata under the broiler for a minute or two at the end of cooking.

Cool and serve. Cool in the pan for 5 minutes, then slice into wedges and serve.

Chicken Breakfast Sausage

4 Servings

These are terrific served alongside a few eggs cooked just the way you like them! These sausage patties are full of traditional flavor!

1 lb ground organic hormone free chicken meat

2 Tbsp. fresh sage leaves, finely minced

1 tsp. fresh thyme leaves, finely chopped

2 tsp. granulated onion

2 tsp. granulated garlic

½ tsp. ground mace

2 tsp. sea salt

Mix all the ingredients together and form 2-3 oz patties. In a nonstick pan, add a little extra virgin olive oil, and fry each patty on both sides until golden brown and internal temperature reaches 165F on your meat thermometer. If the inside is still a little under cooked, you can place the patties on a baking sheet in a 350F oven for a few minutes to complete the cooking process.

Sweet Potato Hash

Serves 2

1 large sweet potato, peeled and diced

4 organic and hormone free eggs, whisked

4 slices sugar and nitrate free bacon

2 cups organic kale leaves finely chopped

1 large organic yellow onion, diced

6 Tbsp. Extra virgin olive oil, divided

Preheat oven to 375F. Line a cookie sheet with parchment. Toss the diced sweet potatoes in 3 Tbsp. of the olive oil and spread out on cookie sheet and roast for 15 minutes or until tender and a little golden brown. Heat the other 3 Tbsp. of olive oil in a nonstick sauté pan and add the onions, sauté until tender. Add the kale and sauté a few more minutes until wilted. Remove mixture to plate and set aside. In same pan, cook bacon strips until crisp, remove from pan and drain on towel. Retain 2 Tbsp. of the bacon fat in the pan and fry the scrambled eggs in it, using a wooden spoon to stir until cooked through. Divide the potatoes onto 2 plates, top with the kale mixture, then the bacon and then the eggs.

Almond Flour Pancakes

2 Servings

I am recommending almond flour pancakes here instead of traditional flour because they are very high in protein and are also gluten free.

1 cup finely milled almond flour

1/2 tsp baking powder

1/4 tsp sea salt

2 organic hormone free eggs

1/4 cup any kind of milk

1 tsp coconut oil, melted and cooled

1 tsp vanilla extract

extra coconut oil for the pan

Mix the dry ingredients together in a bowl.

Mix the wet ingredients together in a bowl.

Pour the dry ingredients into the wet ingredients and mix just until combined.

Heat some oil in a large nonstick skillet on medium heat and pour a ladle of the batter into the pan. Let cook for about 2-3 minutes until little bubbles start to form on top, then flip and let cook for another minute.

Serve pancakes with your favorite toppings like blueberries, yogurt, coconut butter, or maple syrup.

Alongside your egg breakfast or pancakes, please add some additional sides to increase your protein, calorie and nutritional intake. (One funny thing to note is that once you stop drinking alcohol and soda and eliminate the junk food, it actually takes effort to get 2000 calories into your body each day.)

Additional Sides to eat with breakfast:

Roasted organic sweet potatoes

Brown rice, quinoa

Cut up fruit, all kinds, organic

Avocado slices

Tomato slices

Sugar and nitrate free bacon

Snacks to eat any time:

Nut butters, sugar free

Fresh fruits, all types

Vegetables, all types

Legume/Bean salads (recipes below)

Hummus (chapter 2 has a recipe)

Bone broth (chapter 2 has recipes)

Soups, all types (recipes below)

Lunch and Dinner Recipes:

Grilled Salmon Teriyaki

Serves 4

4 (6 oz) wild caught salmon fillets, skin and bones removed

1 green onion, chopped

1/2 tsp sesame seeds, for serving (optional)

Teriyaki Sauce

6 - 8 Tbsp gluten free soy sauce, or coconut aminos

8 Tbsp water divided

3 Tbsp raw honey

1 Tbsp minced organic garlic (3 cloves)

1 Tbsp minced organic fresh ginger

½ Tbsp fresh lemon juice

1 Tbsp cornstarch

Preheat oven to 400 degrees and lightly oil a Pyrex baking dish with olive oil.

In a small saucepan whisk together soy sauce, 6 Tbsp water, honey, garlic, ginger and lemon juice and bring mixture to a light boil over medium heat.

Whisk together cornstarch with remaining 2 Tbsp water, then add to sauce mixture in saucepan.

Let mixture boil, whisking constantly, for 1 minute. Remove from heat and let cool slightly.

Place salmon in baking dish then pour teriyaki sauce evenly over salmon (I also like to lift the fillets up so the sauce runs right under).

Bake in preheated oven 12 – 15 minutes until salmon has cooked through (cooked time will vary depending on thickness of salmon).

Serve warm topped with some of the teriyaki sauce from the baking dish (use excess sauce for steamed asparagus or broccoli on the side) and chopped green onions and sesame seeds.

Creamy Lemon Garlic Parmesan Chicken

Serves 4

4 (6 oz) boneless and skinless chicken breasts

2 tablespoons cornstarch or arrowroot

2 tablespoons finely grated fresh Parmesan cheese

1 teaspoon sea salt

Black pepper

Sauce:

1 tablespoon extra-virgin olive oil

2 teaspoons grass-fed butter (or oil)

2 tablespoons minced organic garlic

1 1/4 cup organic chicken broth

1/2 cup coconut cream or heavy cream

1/3 cup finely grated fresh Parmesan cheese

2 tablespoons capers (plus 2 tablespoons extra to garnish)

1 teaspoon cornstarch mixed with 1 tablespoon of water

2-3 tablespoons fresh lemon juice -- juice of 1 lemon (adjust to your tastes)

2 tablespoons fresh organic parsley

In a shallow bowl, combine the cornstarch and parmesan cheese. Season the chicken with salt and pepper; dredge in the cheese mixture; shake off excess and set aside.

Heat 1 tablespoon of oil and 2 teaspoons butter in a large skillet over medium-high heat until grass-fed butter has melted and pan is hot. Fry the chicken until golden on each side and cooked through and no longer pink (about 3-4 minutes, depending on the thickness of your chicken). Transfer onto a warm plate.

Add the garlic to the oil in the pan (add a little more oil if needed) and fry until fragrant (about 1 minute). Reduce heat to low-medium heat, add the broth and cream.

Bring the sauce to a gentle simmer; season with salt and pepper to your taste; add in the parmesan cheese and capers. Continue cooking gently for about 2 minutes until thicker.

Pour in the lemon juice, allow to simmer for a further minute to combine. Add the chicken back into the pan, allow to simmer gently in the sauce for about a minute to soak up all of the flavors in the sauce.

Serve with the sauce alongside steamed vegetables, zucchini noodles or brown rice. Top with extra capers to garnish, lemon slices and parsley.

Shrimp Scampi

Serves 4

1/2 cup grass-fed butter, cubed

4 cloves organic garlic, minced

2 tablespoons organic shallot or onion, minced

1/4 teaspoon crushed red pepper flakes

1 1/2 pounds wild caught shrimp, peeled and deveined

Sea salt and freshly ground black pepper, to taste

3 tablespoons chopped fresh organic parsley leaves

1 tablespoon freshly squeezed organic lemon juice

2 teaspoons lemon zest

Melt butter in a large skillet over medium heat. Add garlic, shallot and red pepper flakes, and cook, stirring frequently, until fragrant, about 2 minutes.

Add shrimp; season with salt and pepper, to taste. Cook, stirring occasionally, until pink and cooked through, about 3-4 minutes.

Stir in parsley, lemon juice and lemon zest.

Serve immediately over zucchini noodles or with a side of brown or cauliflower rice to soak up all the extra garlic butter.

Apple Chicken Burger with Cranberry Sauce

Serves 3-4

1 lb organic hormone free ground chicken breast

1 organic granny smith apple peeled and diced small

1 Tbsp. fresh rosemary, finely minced

2 Tbsp. diced organic onion, sauteed in olive oil and cooled

4 slices sugar and nitrate free bacon, cooked and finely chopped (reserve bacon fat from pan)

1 tsp. sea salt

Mix all of the ingredients together and form 3 oz patties. Heat the reserved bacon fat or some olive oil in a non-stick sauté pan and fry the patties on both sides until golden brown and cooked through to 165F internal temperature. If they are still undercooked inside, you can transfer them to a baking sheet and finish the cooking process in a 350F oven.

Cranberry Sauce

1 bag fresh or frozen organic cranberries, whole (12 oz)

½ cup pure maple syrup

2 Tbsp. water

Put the cranberries in a saucepan with the water and bring to a simmer. As the heat runs through the cranberries, they will soften and begin to release their juices. Once that happens, add the maple syrup and stir well. Serve the cranberry sauce with the apple chicken patties.

Honey Balsamic Chicken

Serves 4

¼ cup balsamic vinegar

¼ cup extra virgin olive oil

¼ cup raw honey

½ teaspoon dried thyme

½ teaspoon dried rosemary

2 pounds bone-in organic hormone free chicken thighs

ea salt and pepper to taste

Whisk balsamic vinegar, olive oil, honey, thyme, and rosemary together in a bowl until smooth; pour marinade into a resealable plastic bag.

eason chicken thighs with salt and black pepper; add to marinade in plastic bag. queeze bag to remove air and seal. Marinate chicken in refrigerator for 2 to 8 ours. Preheat oven to 375F degrees. Pour chicken and marinade into a baking ish. Bake chicken in preheated oven until no longer pink at the bone and the uices run clear, 35 to 40 minutes. An instant-read thermometer inserted near the one should read 165F degrees.

urkey Meatloaf

erves 3-4

cup almond flour

cup shredded parmesan cheese

organic hormone free eggs

cup organic tomato sauce

organic onion, minced

tablespoon grass-fed butter

pounds ground organic hormone free turkey

teaspoons Italian seasoning

tablespoons parsley chopped

cup organic zucchini or mushrooms, finely shredded

a salt and pepper to taste

Turkey Meatloaf Sauce

2/3 cup organic ketchup or tomato sauce

1 tablespoon organic honey

Preheat oven to 400°F. Line a pan with foil and spray with cooking spray.

Cook onion and butter in a pan until onion is translucent (about 5 minutes). Cool.

In a bowl, combine almond flour, eggs, and tomato sauce. Let sit 5 minutes. Add remaining ingredients and mix just until combined, do not overmix.

Form into a loaf about 4" wide and 3" high. Bake for 35 minutes.

Combine Meatloaf Sauce ingredients. Spread on top and bake an additional 20 minutes or until center of meatloaf reaches 165°F.

Beef Pot Roast

Serves 8

1 tablespoon extra-virgin olive oil

3-4 pounds grass fed chuck roast or rump roast

1 large organic onion chopped, or two small onions

4 organic carrots, peeled and cut into 2" pieces

2 stalks organic celery cut into 1 ½" pieces

1 pound organic baby potatoes, any kind

¼ cup balsamic vinegar

2 cups organic beef broth or as needed

4 cloves organic garlic coarsely chopped

½ teaspoon fresh rosemary, chopped

½ teaspoon fresh thyme, chopped

1 bay leaf

Preheat oven to 300°F.

Season roast with sea salt and pepper.

In a large dutch oven, heat 1 tablespoon olive oil over medium-high heat. Sear the roast on each side until browned, about 4 minutes per side adding more oil if needed.

Arrange onions around the roast. Combine vinegar, broth, rosemary, garlic, and thyme. Pour over the roast. Add bay leaf.

Bring just to a simmer on the stovetop over medium-high heat. Once the broth is simmering, cover and place in the oven and bake 2 hours.

Add potatoes, carrots, and celery, and bake an additional 2 hours (for a 4lb roast) or until the roast and potatoes are fork-tender.

Discard bay leaf. Gently pull beef into large pieces with a fork or slice into thick pieces. Serve with juices (or make gravy below if desired).

To Make Gravy:

Combine 2 tablespoons cornstarch with 2 tablespoons cold water until smooth.

Remove beef and vegetables from the pot and set on a plate to rest. Add extra broth if needed.

Bring broth to a boil and whisk in cornstarch mixture a little bit at a time until thickened.

Season with sea salt & pepper to taste.

Greek Chicken

Serves 4

1 organic red pepper cut into 2-inch pieces

1 organic yellow pepper cut into 2-inch pieces

1 organic red onion cut into eighths

2 cups organic cherry tomatoes

1/2 cup organic artichoke hearts, halved

1 lemon, cut into wedges

4 large organic hormone free chicken breasts, cut in half or 4 chicken thighs

4 cloves organic garlic crushed

1/4 cup extra virgin olive oil

1 1/2 tbsp balsamic vinegar

1/2 tsp smoked paprika

1 tsp dried oregano

1/4 tsp sea salt

1/2 tsp pepper

2 tbsp chopped fresh basil

2/3 cup kalamata olives

1/4 cup chopped feta

Preheat the oven to 400F.

In a large baking sheet or roasting tray, add the chopped peppers, red onion slices, artichoke hearts, lemon wedges and tomatoes.

In a bowl whisk together the garlic, olive oil, vinegar, paprika and oregano. Pour 1/3 of the sauce over the veggies, sprinkle with salt and pepper and toss until well coated. Place the chicken pieces on top of the veggies and brush with sauce. Bake in the oven for 25 minutes.

After 25 minutes, add in the feta, chopped basil and olives. Pour the remaining sauce over the tray and return to the oven to bake for another 5-10 minutes. Check the chicken to ensure its no longer pink.

Asian Glazed Pork Tenderloin

Serves 4-6

1 tablespoon organic honey

2 teaspoons sea salt

1 teaspoon powdered ginger

1/2 teaspoon cinnamon

1 teaspoon garlic powder

1/2 teaspoon powdered cloves

1/4 teaspoon black pepper

2 pounds organic pastured pork tenderloin

For the glaze

1/2 cup honey

1 tablespoon cornstarch

1/4 cup rice vinegar (or organic apple cider vinegar)

1/2 cup cold water

2 tablespoons gluten free soy sauce, or coconut aminos

2 teaspoons fresh organic ginger, minced

fresh cilantro, to garnish

lime wedges, to garnish

In a small bowl, combine the honey, sea salt, powdered ginger, cinnamon, garlic, cloves and black pepper.

Place the tenderloins in the slow cooker. Rub the seasonings over the pork, including the bottom.

Pour ½ cup water in the slow cooker, on the edge or in the middle so that you don't wash off all the spices you just rubbed on.

Cook on low for 6-8 hours, then preheat your broiler.

While the pork is finishing up in the slow cooker and your broiler heats up, combine 1/2 cup honey, cornstarch, rice vinegar, cold water, and soy sauce in a small saucepan.

Set over medium heat and stir until mixture thickens, about 4 minutes.

Remove from heat and stir in minced ginger.

Line a baking sheet with aluminum foil and spray with nonstick spray.

Remove the pork from the crock pot (discard the liquid) and place on the lined baking sheet. Brush a generous amount of the glaze on the pork.

Put your oven rack as high as it will go, and broil the pork for 1 or 2 minutes, until bubbly and caramelized.

Serve with remaining glaze on the side, and garnish with lime and cilantro. This goes well with Cauliflower Fried Rice.

Pork Eggroll Stir fry

Serves 3-4

2 tablespoons toasted sesame oil

3 cloves organic garlic, minced

½ cup organic onion, diced

5 green organic onions, sliced on a bias (white and green parts)

1 pound organic pastured ground pork

½ teaspoon ground ginger

sea salt and black pepper, to taste

1 tsp. red pepper flakes, more to taste

4 cups organic white cabbage cut into thin shreds (like cole slaw)

3 tablespoons Coconut Aminos or gluten free soy sauce

1 tablespoon unseasoned rice vinegar

2 tablespoons toasted sesame seeds

Heat the sesame oil in a large skillet over medium high heat.

Add the garlic, onion, and white portion of the green onions. Sauté until the onions are translucent and the garlic is fragrant.

Add the ground pork, ginger, sea salt, pepper and pepper flakes. Sauté until the pork is cooked through.

Add the cabbage, soy sauce, and rice vinegar. Sauté until the cabbage is tender.

Top with green onions and sesame seeds before serving.

This would go well with brown rice.

Ginger Lime Halibut

Serves 2

2 (6 oz) pieces of wild caught halibut, skin and bones removed

2 tsp. fresh grated organic ginger

2 Tbsp. raw honey

4 Tbsp. fresh lime juice, plus 2 tsp. lime zest

½ cup organic chicken stock or bone broth

3 Tbsp. sliced green onions

2 Tbsp. grass-fed butter

1 Tbsp. cornstarch or arrowroot flour

2 Tbsp. sesame oil

Preheat oven to 350F. Place halibut filets into a small Pyrex dish and season lightly with sea salt and pepper. Top each filet with 1 Tbsp. butter. Bake until fish flakes easily with a fork, approximately 15 minutes. Meanwhile, heat the sesame oil in a nonstick skillet. Sweat the ginger and scallions, add the lime juice, honey and chicken stock. Bring to simmer until reduced by half, dilute the cornstarch in a little water and whisk into the sauce to thicken. Pour over the halibut filets.

Herb Grilled Mahi

Serves 4

4 (6 oz) portions of wild caught Mahi Mahi (skin and bones removed)

1 Tbsp Extra virgin Olive Oil

1/2 tsp Paprika

1 tsp Italian Seasoning

1/2 tsp Garlic Powder

1/2 tsp Sea salt

1/2 tsp Pepper

Mix together the seasoning in a small bowl.

Use a basting brush to rub the olive oil onto the Mahi Mahi filets.

Season the Mahi Mahi with the seasoning mixture.

Heat the grill over medium high heat.

Cook for 3-5 minutes on both sides of the filets until the fish flakes with a fork.

Ropa Vieja with Brown Rice

Serves 6

1.5 lbs. of grass-fed skirt steak flank steak, or top sirloin

1 organic onion sliced

1 organic carrot sliced into chunks

1 organic red or orange bell pepper sliced into strips

6 cloves organic garlic minced or pressed

1 tsp sea salt

1 tsp ground cumin

2 cups organic beef broth

2 cups organic tomato sauce

2 tsp oregano

1 tsp black pepper

2/3 cup frozen peas

Place meat in the bottom of the slow cooker.

Add all spices and broth on top

Add vegetables (except for the peas).

Top with tomato sauce.

Cook on low for 8-10 hours.

Boil peas for 4-5 minutes and add to the slow cooker.

Shred meat and serve over brown rice.

Salmon Burgers with Guacamole

Serves 3

Burgers:

lb boneless skinless wild caught fresh salmon

Tbsp. fresh chopped dill

Tbsp. minced red onion

Tbsp. minced fresh garlic

tsp. fresh lemon zest

tsp. sea salt

tsp. pepper

Tbsp. extra virgin olive oil

Guacamole:

ripe organic Haas avocadoes

Juice of 1 fresh organic lime

Tbsp. fresh chopped cilantro

clove fresh organic garlic minced

tsp. sea salt

Using a sharp knife, finely chop the salmon until it is a mince. If you happen to own a meat grinder, you can put the salmon through the grinder as an alternative. Combine the salmon with all of the other ingredients except the olive oil. Form the mixture into 6 patties. Heat the oil in a nonstick sauté pan, fry the patties in the oil until golden brown on each side, and just cooked through. Don't overcook they may become dry.

For the guacamole, remove the flesh from the avocadoes and mash in a small bowl with the other ingredients. Serve the guacamole on top of the burgers.

The salmon burgers pair well with zucchini noodles a big green garden salad or cauliflower rice.

Shrimp Pad Thai with Veggie Noodles

Serves 2

If you don't have a spiralized or don't want to do that step, most grocery stores offer some variety of pre-spiralized vegetables. You can use any combination you like. The Pad Thai sauce I've offered here is a healthier, sugar free and MSG free alternative with great flavor.

1 lb raw wild caught shrimp peeled and deveined

2 Tbsp. minced organic garlic

2 Tbsp. extra virgin olive oil

Sauce:

1 oz tamarind paste

1 oz organic fish sauce

1 oz gluten free soy sauce or coconut aminos

2 cups sugar free pineapple juice

1 Tbsp. arrowroot powder or cornstarch

Noodles:

1 organic rutabaga, peeled and spiralized into noodles

1 cup organic green cabbage, cut into ribbons

1 organic carrot, peeled and spiralized

1 small organic zucchini, spiralized into noodles

1 tsp. sea salt

3 Tbsp. extra virgin olive oil or coconut oil

2 Tbsp. thinly sliced scallions (for garnish)

In a small saucepan, add the pineapple juice and simmer until reduced by half (to 1 cup), add the other ingredients (except arrowroot) and bring to simmer again. Dilute the arrowroot or cornstarch in a little water and whisk into the simmering sauce to lightly thicken it. Set aside.

In a large non-stick skillet, add 2 tablespoons of 2 tablespoons of extra virgin olive oil. Once it starts to sizzle, add the cleaned shrimp and sauté until cooked through. Set shrimp aside on a plate and add 3 tablespoons of olive oil, bring to heat, then add whatever vegetable noodles you are using, sprinkle with the salt and sauté turning frequently with tongs until noodles are just starting to soften up, but aren't mushy. Serve the shrimp over the noodles drizzled with the pad Thai sauce. Sprinkle with some sliced scallions.

Garlic Chicken and Broccoli Casserole

Serves 4

1 Tbsp. extra virgin olive oil or avocado oil

1 lb organic, hormone free boneless skinless chicken breast

20 oz organic broccoli florets

1 cup heavy cream or full fat coconut cream

1/2 cup parmesan cheese

2 cloves minced organic garlic

1 tsp. sea salt

1 cup mozzarella cheese

Cut chicken into bite sized cubes. Preheat oil in a nonstick skillet. Add pieces of chicken and cook it until golden brown. Pour into a Pyrex baking dish.

Cut broccoli florets into bite-size pieces. Add them to the dish with chicken.

Combine cream, parmesan cheese, salt and garlic together. Pour the sauce over the broccoli.

Bake at 350F for 10 minutes. Remove from the oven and sprinkle the mozzarella cheese on top.

Bake for 7 more minutes or until the cheese gets slightly golden. Serve right away while the cheese is still all melted.

Serve over brown rice or cauliflower rice.

Optional: If you wanted a crunchy topping for your casserole, there is a great product called Pork Panko. It is essentially pasture raised pork cracklings that are ground into a panko textured crumb. It holds up well to breading and frying cutlets, topping casseroles and anything else you'd generally do with Panko. It's available online.

Snapper Provençale

Serves 4

2–3 medium organic shallots, chopped

4 oz sliced organic mushrooms

1 cup diced organic tomatoes

1 clove organic garlic minced

1/3 cup pitted Kalamata olives

1/3 cup white wine vinegar or organic apple cider vinegar

2 1/2 teaspoons capers

1 teaspoon sea salt

½ teaspoon ground black pepper

1 1/2 pounds wild caught boneless skinless snapper fillets

Chop shallots and place in medium bowl. Stir in mushrooms, tomatoes, olives, garlic vinegar and capers.

Preheat large non-stick sauté pan on medium-high 2–3 minutes. Place remaining 2 tablespoons olive oil in pan; swirl to coat. Season fish with sea salt and pepper; place in pan. Cook 2–3 minutes on each side or until golden.

Pour tomato mixture over fish; reduce to medium and cook 4–5 minutes, stirring often, or just until fish is opaque and separates easily with a fork.

This dish would pair well with roasted brussels sprouts.

Artichoke and Asparagus Seafood Gratin

Serves 2

3 cloves garlic

⅛ bunch organic Italian parsley

6 oz canned artichoke hearts

1 organic lemon

2 tablespoons unsalted grass-fed butter, divided

½ cup Pork Panko crumbs

1 tablespoon arrowroot powder or cornstarch

¼ cup organic chicken stock

½ cup heavy whipping cream

1 teaspoon Greek seasoning, divided

2 (6 oz) wild caught white fish fillets (such as cod, haddock, or tilapia; about 12 oz)

4 oz fresh organic asparagus tips

Preheat oven to 400°F. Slice garlic thinly; chop parsley coarsely (2 tablespoons). Drain artichokes; juice one-half lemon (1 tablespoon) and cut remaining half into wedges. Melt 1 tablespoon butter and toss with pork panko and parsley.

Preheat medium, nonstick sauté pan on medium 2–3 minutes. Add remaining 1 tablespoon butter and garlic; cook 2–3 minutes, stirring occasionally, or until garlic is softened and fragrant. Stir in cornstarch and cook 1 minute, stirring often. Add stock, cream, 1/2 teaspoon seasoning, and lemon juice; cook 2–3 minutes or until sauce has thickened.

Pour cream mixture into 9-inch-square baking dish. Nestle fish, asparagus, and artichokes into cream mixture. Sprinkle with remaining 1/2 teaspoon seasoning and top with panko mixture. Bake 10–12 minutes until topping is browned and fish opaque and flakes easily. Serve with lemon wedges.

Cook to an internal temperature of 145°F.

This dish would pair well with brown rice.

Trout Almondine

Serves 2

2 whole wild caught rainbow trout (or 4 pre-sliced fillets)

1 tablespoon organic shallot, very finely diced

1 teaspoon fresh thyme, chopped

½ cup cornstarch

Sea salt and freshly ground pepper

5 tablespoons unsalted grass-fed butter, divided

2 teaspoons chopped fresh parsley

1/4 cup sliced almonds

2-4 fresh organic lemon wedges

Cut your trout into fillets if they aren't already. In a dish large enough to fit the fillets, mix the cornstarch, finely minced shallots, and thyme; and season generously with salt and pepper. Stir to combine. Press the trout fillets into cornstarch mixture and pat onto both sides to coat completely.

Heat 2 tablespoons of butter in the largest sauté pan or skillet you have, over medium-high heat. When the butter stops bubbling, try to place all four of the fillets in the pan, skin side down. If you have to do them in stages it's fine. Saute the fillets for about 3 minutes, watching carefully that they're nicely browned but not burned. Turn the fillets over and cook them for about 3 minutes more. Transfer the fish to warm plates while making the sauce.

Add the remaining 3 tablespoons of butter and cook over high heat until it stops bubbling and turns a nutty brown. Add the sliced almonds and stir until just barely toasted. Remove the pan from the heat and allow to cool for a few seconds. Toss in the parsley and a little salt and pepper and stir to combine. Pour everything over the trout fillets and squeeze with a bit of fresh lemon juice. Serve immediately, with lemon wedges, mashed sweet potatoes, and sautéed green beans if desired.

Lamb Burgers with Spinach and Feta

Serves 3

1 lb ground grass fed lamb

2 Tbsp. finely chopped organic rosemary

2 tsp. fresh lemon zest

2 cloves organic garlic, minced

1 tsp. sea salt

½ tsp. black pepper

2 cups finely chopped fresh organic spinach

½ cup crumbled feta cheese

2 Tbsp. extra virgin olive oil

Mix all ingredients except oil together in a bowl. Form 3 burger patties from the meat. Heat the oil in a nonstick sauté pan. When pan is hot, fry the burgers on both sides until golden brown. Transfer the burgers to a cookie sheet and bake in the oven until an internal temperature of 155F is reached.

The lamb burgers would pair well with roasted root vegetables.

Herb Roast Whole Chicken

Serves 4

1 whole 3-4 lb organic hormone free chicken

2 Tbsp. fresh organic rosemary, chopped

1 Tbsp. fresh organic sage, chopped

1 Tbsp. fresh organic thyme, chopped

2 tsp. sea salt

1 tsp. black pepper

3 Tbsp. grass-fed butter softened or extra virgin olive oil

Preheat oven to 375F. Use a roasting pan with a rack insert to roast the chicken so that air can circulate around it and cook it evenly.

Dry the chicken with paper towel. Rub the butter or olive oil over the entire chicken to coat. Sprinkle the herbs, salt and pepper evenly over the entire bird.

Place on rack and roast in oven for 1 hour. Remove and temp the chicken at the deepest part of the thigh with your instant read meat thermometer. You are looking for 165F. If not done yet, take this opportunity to baste the chicken with any pan juices that may have dripped off during cooking. Put back in the oven and check again in 15 minutes. Try not to overcook, as the meat will be dry. If you temp the chicken and it reads 163F, go ahead and take it out because the carry over cooking will bring it up to the 165F. Tent the chicken and let it rest a few minutes before cutting so that the juices don't come pouring out.

This chicken is great with mashed sweet potatoes and creamed spinach.

Orange Chicken with Stir fry Veggies

Serves 3

1 lb. boneless skinless organic hormone free chicken breast, cut into bite sized pieces

3 Tbsp. extra virgin olive oil

½ cup fresh orange juice, (squeezed from organic oranges)

1 Tbsp. orange zest (from your organic oranges)

3 Tbsp. coconut aminos (or gluten free soy sauce)

1 Tbsp. raw honey

1 Tbsp. organic apple cider vinegar

1 tsp. fresh minced ginger

2 tsp. fresh minced garlic

1 Tbsp. arrowroot powder or cornstarch

3 organic scallions, thinly sliced

In a nonstick skillet, heat the olive oil. Cook the chicken pieces until fully cooked. Remove from pan and set aside. Add a little more oil, then add the ginger and garlic. Sauté until fragrant. Add the orange juice, zest, aminos, honey, and vinegar. Bring to simmer. Dilute the arrowroot or cornstarch in a little water and whisk into the orange sauce to thicken. Add the chicken back to the pan with the sauce and stir to coat. Sprinkle with scallions and serve.

This dish pairs well with cauliflower fried rice.

Chicken Pineapple Curry

Serves 3

This dish can be made with your favorite curry powder blend, or you can whip up a quick batch of my anti-inflammatory curry powder (recipe below). Curry is so beneficial because it has both turmeric and ginger which are powerful anti-inflammatory ingredients.

1 lb organic hormone free chicken breast (boneless, skinless), cut into bite sized pieces

2 Tbsp. curry powder (see recipe below)

1 can full fat coconut milk

1 cup fresh organic pineapple diced

1 small organic onion, diced

2 Tbsp. fresh organic lime juice

2 tsp. fresh minced organic ginger

1 Tbsp. fresh organic minced garlic

3 Tbsp. extra virgin coconut oil

1 Tbsp. organic honey

1 Tbsp. arrowroot powder or cornstarch

1 tsp. sea salt

1 Tbsp. fresh chopped cilantro

Heat oil in large non-stick skillet. Add onions and sauté until translucent. Add ginger and garlic. Sauté until fragrant. Add chicken pieces. Sprinkle with curry powder and salt. Stir well, then add the lime juice, honey and coconut milk. Bring to simmer. And cook until chicken is cooked through. Dilute the arrowroot in a little water and stir in to thicken the sauce. Fold in the pineapple at the end. Sprinkle with the cilantro.

This dish pairs well with cilantro lime coconut rice.

Curry Powder

2 Tbsp. granulated garlic

2 Tbsp. granulated onion

2 Tbsp. turmeric

1 Tbsp. cinnamon

1 tsp. powdered ginger

½ tsp. ground cloves

Herb Crusted Roast Pork Loin

Serves 6

Herb and Mustard Crust:

4 tbsp coarse grain organic Dijon mustard

3 cloves organic garlic minced

2 tbsp. chopped fresh thyme

2 tbsp dry oregano

1 tbsp coarsely ground black pepper

1 tbsp chopped fresh rosemary

1 tbsp coconut aminos

1 tsp sea salt

3 lb or more pastured pork loin roast

Mix together all of the ingredients for the Herb and Mustard Crust into a paste.

Rub paste over the entire surface of the pork loin roast.

Roast uncovered on a rack in a large roasting pan at 350 degrees F for about 20 minutes per pound or until internal temperature of the roast reaches 160 degrees F on a meat thermometer.

Allow roast to rest for 15 minutes after it comes out of the oven before carving and serving.

This roast pairs well with baked apples and onions and roasted sweet potatoes.

Salisbury Steak with Mushroom Gravy

Serves 3

Steaks:

1 lb grass fed ground beef, bison, buffalo or elk meat

3 Tbsp. finely minced organic onions

2 cloves minced organic garlic

2 Tbsp. finely chopped organic parsley

1 tsp. sea salt

½ tsp. ground black pepper

2 Tbsp. extra virgin olive oil

Gravy:

2 cups organic beef bone broth

8 oz sliced organic mushrooms

1 small organic onion sliced

2 Tbsp. extra virgin olive oil

1 tsp. sea salt

½ tsp. ground black pepper

First, get the steaks ready. Mix all of the steak ingredients together except the oil. Form into 3 oval patties. Heat the oil in a nonstick sauté pan. Fry the steaks on each side until nice and brown. They will still be raw inside. Set aside. Heat the other 2 tablespoons of oil in the pan, and add the sliced onions, cook stirring frequently until they start to caramelize. Add the mushrooms, bone broth, salt and pepper and bring to simmer. Dilute the arrowroot or cornstarch in a little water and whisk to thicken. Keep sauce simmering and add the steaks and any juices that may have run off them into the gravy. Lower heat and cover. Cook the steaks for 8-10 minutes until cooked through.

Pairs well with roasted root vegetables, cauliflower mash and a green salad.

Moo Shu Pork Lettuce Wraps

Serves 4

1 pound pastured pork tenderloin

1/2 tsp baking soda

1 1/2 tbsp coconut aminos

1 tbsp apple cider vinegar

1 1/2 tbsp sesame oil

2 organic hormone free eggs

7 ounces organic shiitake mushrooms stems removed and cut into thin slices

1 large organic carrot shredded or julienned

2 1/2 cups shredded organic savoy cabbage

1 cup shredded organic red cabbage

1/3 cup sliced organic scallions

1 tbsp finely minced organic ginger

4 cloves garlic finely minced

Sauce:

4 large medjool dates soaked in hot water for 10 minutes

1 tbsp chopped ginger

1 tbsp almond butter

2 tbsp coconut aminos

1 tbsp balsamic vinegar

1 tbsp apple cider vinegar

1/2 tsp Chinese 5 spice

To Serve

1 head organic butter lettuce or iceberg lettuce

2 tbsp chopped organic scallions

1 tsp sesame seeds

Cut the pork tenderloin into thin strips and place them in a bowl. Add the baking soda, apple cider vinegar and coconut aminos to the bowl and leave to marinate while you chop the veggies and prepare the sauce.

In a high-speed blender combine the drained medjool dates, ginger, almond butter, coconut aminos, balsamic vinegar, apple cider vinegar and Chinese 5 spice and blend into a thick paste like sauce. If the mixture is too thick to blend add a splash of water. Once completely blended, transfer to a small bowl and set aside.

Heat 1/2 tbsp sesame oil in a large nonstick skillet on medium high heat. Whisk the eggs in a bowl and pour them into the skillet. Leave the eggs to cook untouched for approximately 3 minutes until they are set (like an omelet). Slide the omelet from the skillet onto a cutting board and chop into thin small strips. Set aside.

Add the sliced pork plus any excess marinade to the skillet and cook for approximately 4 minutes until the pork is golden in color and cooked through. Transfer the cooked pork to a plate.

Add the remaining 1 tbsp of sesame oil to the skillet and once hot add in the garlic and ginger and cook for 1 minute until fragrant. Add in the shredded cabbage, carrots, shiitake mushrooms and scallions and cook for approximately 4-5 minutes until the cabbage begins to soften.

Once the cabbage has softened (be careful not to overcook!) add in 1 large spoonful of the hoisin sauce plus the cooked pork and stir to combine. Once well mixed add in the strips of eggs and give it a gentle stir with a spatula so as not to break up the egg. Remove from the heat.

Serve the mixture in lettuce cups and garnish with a drizzle of the hoisin sauce and a sprinkle of chopped scallions.

Tom Kha Gai Soup

Serves 4

1 tablespoon extra-virgin coconut oil

1 small organic onion sliced

3 cloves organic garlic chopped

1/2 of one red jalapeno pepper sliced, or a couple Thai chiles, halved

4 4-inch slices organic ginger

1 organic lemongrass stalk pounded with the side of a knife and cut into 2-inch long pieces

1 tablespoon curry powder

4 cups organic chicken broth

4 cups canned coconut cream or coconut milk

1 lb organic hormone free chicken breasts cut into bite-sized pieces, or 1 lb wild caught peeled and deveined shrimp

8 ounces organic white mushroom caps sliced

1-2 tablespoons coconut aminos

1 ½ – 2 tablespoons organic fish sauce plus more to taste

2-3 tablespoons fresh organic lime juice

2-3 organic green onions sliced thin

Fresh organic cilantro chopped, for garnish

In a medium pot, heat the coconut oil over medium heat. Add the onion, garlic, jalapeno or chile, ginger, lemongrass, and curry powder and cook, stirring frequently, for 5 minutes, or until onions are softened. Add chicken broth and bring to a boil. Reduce heat and simmer uncovered for 30 minutes.

Strain out the aromatics (the garlic, onions, lemongrass, and ginger) and discard. Add in coconut cream or milk, chicken breast (or shrimp), and mushrooms. Simmer until chicken breast pieces are just cooked through, then add fish sauce, coconut aminos, and lime juice, plus more of each to taste.

Cook 2 minutes, then ladle into serving bowls and top with sliced green onions and fresh cilantro.

Sides:

Creamed Brussels Sprouts

4 Servings

1 lb fresh organic brussels sprouts, sliced thin

1 small organic onion, diced

1 can full fat coconut milk

4 slices sugar and nitrate free bacon, cooked and crumbled

1 tsp. fresh thyme chopped

2 cloves organic garlic minced

3 Tbsp. extra virgin olive oil

Heat the olive oil in a large nonstick skillet. Add the onions and garlic until fragrant, then add the sliced brussels sprouts and sauté until they start to wilt. Add the coconut milk and the chopped thyme. Simmer over low heat until brussels sprouts are tender. Add crumbled bacon at the end to garnish. Add a little salt to taste if needed.

Collard Greens

6 Servings

2 lbs organic collard greens, washed, chopped, stems removed

2 cups organic chicken stock

5 slices sugar and nitrate free bacon, chopped

2 small organic onion, diced

In a large stockpot, put the raw chopped bacon and cook stirring frequently, until crisp. Remove bacon and set aside. Leave bacon fat in the pot. Add the onions and cook until translucent. Add the washed collard greens and the broth and bring to a simmer. Stir well, and cover. Turn heat to low. Cook for at least an hour until greens are very tender. Add crisp cooked bacon at the end.

Roasted Root Vegetables

Servings

4 organic carrots, peeled and cut into bite sized pieces

2 organic sweet potatoes, peeled and large diced

1 large organic beet, peeled and diced

2 organic onions, diced

Keep each vegetable separate. Preheat oven to 375F. Toss the vegetables in extra virgin olive oil or avocado oil to coat and spread out on parchment lined sheet trays. Sprinkle lightly with sea salt and roast until light brown on the edges and tender. Each vegetable will have a slightly different cooking time, so check at 20 minutes and then every few minutes thereafter until all of the vegetables are done. Remove all from oven and mix them together for serving. Other vegetables you may want to mix into this dish would be parsnips, butternut squash (it's not a root vegetable, but it goes well). You can add some chopped rosemary if you like, or sprinkle with some granulated garlic if you like.

Cauliflower Mash

3 Servings

1 head organic cauliflower

3 Tbsp. grass-fed butter

1 tsp. sea salt

1 tsp. granulated garlic (optional)

Break the cauliflower down into florets, discarding the core and leaves. Place into a pot and cover with water. Simmer over medium heat until tender. Remove cauliflower and drain well. Lay out on a tray and dry it in a 350F oven for 5 minutes. (This makes a much fluffier, less watery mash). After removing from oven, add the butter, salt and garlic and mash either by hand or with an immersion blender for a very creamy result.

Roasted Brussels

3 Servings

1 lb organic fresh brussels sprouts

4 Tbsp. extra virgin olive oil

1 tsp. sea salt

1 tsp. granulated garlic

Preheat oven to 375F. Cut brussels sprouts in half, remove any brown core edges or leaves. Toss in olive oil and spread out on parchment lined tray. Sprinkle with sea salt and granulated garlic. Roast until golden brown on one side. Remove from oven and use tongs to flip them over and brown the other side.

Cauliflower Fried Rice

-3 Servings

head organic cauliflower

small yellow onion

Tbsp. Extra virgin olive oil

cup organic peas

cup organic carrot small diced

Tbsp. minced organic fresh ginger

Tbsp. minced organic fresh garlic

Tbsp. sliced organic scallions

Tbsp. gluten free soy sauce or coconut aminos

tsp. sesame oil

ea salt

Trim leaves and stem from cauliflower and break into florets. Put florets one handful at a time into the bowl of a food processor and pulse a few times until rice sized pieces are formed. Scrape each batch into a bowl until it is all processed. Mince the onion very finely. In a large non-stick sauté pan, heat the olive oil and sesame oil together, add the onion, carrots, garlic and ginger and sweat until soft, add the cauliflower rice and peas and stir frequently. Add a few tablespoons of water then cover to let the rice steam for 2 minutes. Remove cover add the soy sauce or coconut aminos and stir and then season to taste with sea salt.

Cilantro Coconut Rice

3-4 Servings

1 head organic cauliflower, core removed, processed into rice

2 Tbsp. extra virgin coconut oil

½ cup full fat coconut milk

3 Tbsp. chopped fresh organic cilantro

2 Tbsp. fresh organic lime juice

2 Tbsp. organic honey (optional)

1 small organic onion, minced

1 tsp. sea salt

Heat the coconut oil in a large nonstick skillet. Add onions, stirring for a minute or two, then add the cauliflower rice. Stir around to sauté for 5 minutes. Add coconut milk, lime juice, honey, sea salt, and cilantro and stir until rice is fully cooked and liquid has been mostly absorbed.

Broccoli Rice

3-4 Servings

1 head organic broccoli

1 small yellow onion, minced

2 cloves organic garlic, minced

3 Tbsp. Extra virgin olive oil

1 tsp. sea salt

Remove leaves and tough stems from broccoli. Break into florets and put into bowl of food processor. Pulse to form small pieces of broccoli "rice." Remove rice to bowl. Heat olive oil in a nonstick sauté pan. Add the onions and garlic. Add the broccoli rice, stir to coat. Add a few tablespoons of water then cover broccoli rice to steam for 2 minutes. Uncover, stir and remove from heat.

Cauliflower Polenta

4 Servings

1 organic head cauliflower, core and leaves removed, processed into rice

1 small organic onion, minced

2 cloves organic garlic, minced

1 cup coconut cream or heavy cream

1 cup cheddar cheese, grated

1 tsp. sea salt

3 Tbsp. extra virgin olive oil, or avocado oil or red palm oil

Heat the oil in a large nonstick skillet. Add the onion and garlic and stir until it is sizzling. Add the cauliflower rice and stir well to combine. Add the cream and sea salt turn heat to low and cover the pan. Simmer for about 10 minutes to reduce the liquid. When the liquid has mostly evaporated, stir in the cheese.

Creamed Spinach

2-3 Servings

1 lb organic baby spinach fresh

1 cup coconut cream or heavy cream

2 cloves organic garlic

1 tsp. sea salt

1 Tbsp. extra virgin olive oil

Heat the oil in a large nonstick skillet, add the garlic and stir until fragrant. Add the spinach and sprinkle with salt. Cook until just done 1-2 minutes. Drain off all excess liquid. Add the cream and bring to simmer. Simmer until thickened and creamy 2-3 minutes.

Mashed Carrots

2-3 servings

1 lb organic carrots, (thin ones, not the thick juicing ones)

3 Tbsp. grass-fed butter

1 tsp. sea salt

1 Tbsp. organic honey

Peel and rough chop the carrots. Put into a small saucepan and cover with water. Bring to simmer. Cook until tender. Drain well, add the butter, sea salt and honey, and mash using hand masher or immersion blender.

Glazed Carrots

2-3 servings

1 lb organic carrots, (thin ones, not the thick juicing ones)

3 Tbsp. grass-fed butter

1 tsp. sea salt

1 Tbsp. organic honey

Peel the carrots and cut into bite sized rounds. Place in a small saucepan and cover with water. Bring to simmer. Cook until tender. Drain well. In a small sauté pan, melt butter and add honey. Bring to simmer. Add cooked carrots and toss well to coat. Season to taste with the sea salt.

Roasted Butternut Squash

3-4 Servings

1 whole organic butternut squash, peeled and seeds removed

4 Tbsp. extra virgin olive oil or avocado oil

1 tsp. sea salt

Preheat oven to 375F. Chop the peeled seeded squash into 1" cubes. Toss in the oil and spread out in an even layer on a parchment lined sheet tray. Sprinkle with the salt. Roast for 20-25 minutes, until just golden around the edges and tender.

Roasted Acorn Squash

2 Servings

Acorn squash is not something you eat very often, yet it's very easy to get. Besides just eating it as a side dish, you can roast the halves and then stuff them with all kinds of cooked meat fillings for an elegant meal.

medium organic acorn squash

tsp. extra virgin olive oil

Preheat oven to 375F. Cut the acorn squash across its middle leaving the stem on the top half. Scoop out the seeds and brush the cut edges with the oil. Place cut side down on a parchment lined sheet tray and roast in the oven for approximately 40 minutes until the skin can be pierced with a sharp knife and you can feel that the squash is tender inside. Remove from oven and tip the squash to the side to release the steam.

Zucchini Noodles

Servings

medium organic zucchini squash

tsp. sea salt

Tbsp. extra virgin olive oil

1 clove organic garlic minced

Using a vegetable spiralizer, cut the ends of each zucchini and run them through the linguini blade to create the noodles. Heat the oil in a large nonstick sauté pan. Add the garlic and when it begins sizzling, add the noodles. Sprinkle with the sea salt and use tongs to turn the noodles to lightly cook them all over. Don't overcook or they become mushy and fall apart.

Butternut Noodles

3 Servings

1 medium organic butternut squash

3 Tbsp. extra virgin coconut oil

1 tsp. sea salt

Cut ends off squash. Peel and remove round bulb end for another use (you can chop it up and freeze it). Discard seeds. Using only the tubular top part of the squash, run it through the spiralizer on the linguini or fettucine setting to create the noodles. Heat the oil in a large nonstick sauté pan. Add the noodles and sprinkle lightly with salt. Use tongs to toss the noodles so that they cook evenly all over. These are incredible with a rich meat sauce over them.

Spaghetti Squash

Serves 2-3

Once you know the secret to cooking perfect spaghetti squash, you'll probably do it a lot more often.

1 organic spaghetti squash (any size)

3 cups hot water in a spouted measuring cup

Cut the squash straight across the middle leaving the stem on the top piece. Scoop all of the seeds out of each half. Preheat oven to 375F. Lay each squash half cut side down on a rimmed sheet tray and place into hot oven. Pour the hot water into the sheet tray. Carefully tip each squash half up to let a little water get underneath. This will create the steam inside each half to cook the spaghetti strands properly. Cook 35-40 minutes. When a sharp knife can pierce through the skin to the tender inside, it is done. Remove tray carefully in case there is any water left that didn't evaporate. Turn both halves over to release the steam. This is important so that the squash doesn't get soggy and mushy. When the squash is cool enough to handle, use a tablespoon or a scoop to remove all of the spaghetti strands from inside of each shell.

Brown Rice

4 Servings

1 cup organic brown rice

2 ½ cups water

Place water and rice in a small saucepan and bring to low simmer. Cover and simmer for 40 minutes or until all water is absorbed.

Brown Fried Rice

4 Servings

3 cups cold cooked brown rice (do not use freshly cooked hot rice)

2 Tbsp. extra virgin olive oil

2 tsp. sesame oil

½ cup organic green peas

½ cup organic carrots, small diced

½ cup organic onion, diced

2 cloves organic garlic minced

1 Tbsp. organic ginger minced

4 Tbsp. thin sliced organic scallions

2 organic hormone free eggs, whisked

4 Tbsp. gluten free soy sauce or coconut aminos

Heat both oils in a large nonstick skillet. Add the ginger, carrots, garlic and onions and sauté until translucent. Add the rice and green peas and stir well. Create a well in the center of the rice and pour in the eggs. Stir them to scramble. Once they are completely cooked, fold them into the rice. Pour in the coconut aminos or gluten free soy sauce.

Creamed Swiss Chard

2-3 Servings

1 lb organic green chard fresh, chopped all stems removed

1 cup coconut cream or heavy cream

2 cloves organic garlic

1 tsp. sea salt

1 Tbsp. extra virgin olive oil

Heat the oil in a large nonstick skillet, add the garlic and stir until fragrant. Add the chard and sprinkle with salt. Cook until just done 1-2 minutes. Drain off all excess liquid. Add the cream and bring to simmer. Simmer until thickened and creamy 2-3 minutes.

Plantain Pilaf

2-3 Servings

2 large green unripe organic plantains (don't use ripe yellow ones)

2 Tbsp. extra virgin olive oil

½ tsp. sea salt

2 tsp. minced organic garlic

2 Tbsp. minced organic onion

Cut the peels off the plantains. (Green plantains won't peel like a banana. The peels are most likely going to need to be cut off). Cut into chunks and process in processor until the size of large rice grains. Heat the oil in a large nonstick skillet. Add the onion and garlic and stir until it sizzles. Add the plantain grains. Stir well to coat with oil. Add a little water and a sprinkle of salt. Stir well and keep cooking. When it turns bright yellow, it is done. This dish has a nutty toasty flavor.

Roasted Garlic White Sweet Potato Mash

3 Servings

1 head organic garlic

3 white organic Japanese sweet potatoes

½ cup coconut cream or heavy cream

1 tsp. sea salt

Preheat oven to 350. Cut top off the garlic head to expose tops of each clove. Wrap in foil and bake for 35-40 minutes until very soft. Meanwhile, peel and rough chop the potatoes. Put into a saucepan and cover with water. Simmer until tender, about 20 minutes. Drain well. Mash with cream and sea salt. When garlic is cooled, squeeze it from the bottom to release all of the roasted garlic from inside their skins directly into the potatoes. Mash it in thoroughly.

Sauteed Garlic Kale

3-4 Servings

1 lb organic kale stems removed washed and finely chopped

3 cloves organic garlic minced

1 Tbsp. extra virgin olive oil

1 tsp. sea salt

In a large nonstick skillet, heat the oil, add the garlic, when it starts sizzling, then add the kale and a little water. Cover and steam until wilted, sprinkle with salt and stir until completely cooked about 5 minutes.

Quinoa

Serves 2-3

1 cup white organic quinoa

2 cups water

In a fine mesh strainer, put the dry quinoa and rinse it well under running water for a few minutes. This will remove any residual bitterness. Pour washed quinoa into a small saucepan and add 2 cups of water. Bring to low simmer. Cover and cook for approximately 20 minutes until all water absorbed. Remove lid and fluff lightly with a fork.

Lemony Lentil and Quinoa Salad

6 Servings

1 cup organic white quinoa

2 cloves garlic, peeled and smashed

½ cup lentils, rinsed well (Le Puy green lentils are great here)

bay leaf

Sea salt and freshly ground black pepper

1 tsp ground cumin

½ tsp ground coriander

ground cinnamon

¼ cup organic lemon juice (freshly squeezed is best)

¼ cup extra virgin olive oil

1 tsp grated lemon zest

½ cup flat-leaf parsley, chopped fine

½ cup fresh mint, chopped fine

2 small organic English cucumbers, peeled, seeded, and diced

1 cup diced organic tomato, (or cherry tomatoes, halved)

small handful of currants

2 Tbsp crumbled feta

Quinoa:

In a fine mesh sieve, rinse the quinoa until the water runs clear; drain and transfer to a medium pot.

Add 2 cups water, a garlic clove, and a pinch of sea salt. Bring to a boil. Cover, reduce heat, and simmer until the water has absorbed (about 20 minutes).

Remove from heat and let stand 5 minutes (Quinoa should be tender enough to eat, but with a little "pop" upon biting into it)

Add the cumin, coriander, and a small pinch of cinnamon. Fluff with a fork until well combined. Set aside to cool.

Lentils:

Meanwhile, in a pot over medium-high heat, add the lentils, the other garlic clove, bay leaf, and a pinch of sea salt. Cover with about 2 inches of water.

Bring to a boil before reducing the heat; let the lentils simmer until they're tender (about 20-25 minutes). Drain, discarding the bay leaf and garlic. Spritz with a squeeze of lemon juice before setting them aside to cool.

Lemony Dressing:

In a small bowl, whisk together the lemon juice, olive oil, lemon zest, and a small pinch of sea salt.

Salad:

Combine the quinoa, lentils, mint, and parsley. Drizzle with lemony dressing and fluff with a fork.

Chill for at least 2 hours.

Before serving, add the tomatoes, cucumber, and currants; along with a sprinkling of feta.

Three Bean Salad

6 Servings

15 oz. cooked organic kidney beans

15 oz. cooked organic black beans

15 oz. cooked organic cannellini beans

1 medium organic celery rib

½ medium organic onion

1 small bunch of parsley

For the dressing:

3 tbsp. extra virgin olive oil

1 tbsp. organic apple cider vinegar or lemon juice

½ tsp. sea salt

½ tsp. cumin powder

2 garlic cloves, minced

a pinch of cayenne

Prep the veggies and beans. Dice the celery, onions, and parsley. Set aside. Thoroughly rinse the three beans and also set aside.

Make the dressing. Add the olive oil, vinegar, minced garlic, cumin, salt, and a pinch of cayenne to a small mason jar and shake well until all the ingredients are well incorporated.

Make the Salad. Place all three beans into a large bowl. Then, add the chopped celery, onions, and parsley. Pour the dressing on top and mix well until everything is coated in dressing

Kale Caesar Salad with Crispy Parmesan Chickpeas

Serves 4

For the Crispy Parmesan Roasted Chickpeas:

1 15 oz. can organic chickpeas

1 Tbsp extra virgin olive oil

½ tsp garlic powder

½ tsp grated lemon zest

Sea salt and freshly ground pepper to taste

2 Tbsp grated Parmesan cheese

For the Salad:

4 cups chopped fresh organic kale stems removed

1 Tbsp extra virgin olive oil

1 Tbsp organic lemon juice

pinch of sea salt

4 cups chopped organic Romaine lettuce

¼ cup grated Parmesan cheese

For the Caesar Dressing:

1 Tbsp extra virgin olive oil

¾ cup plain Greek yogurt

3 Tbsp grated Parmesan cheese

2 Tbsp fresh lemon juice approximately the juice of one medium organic lemon

1 Tbsp Dijon mustard

1 tsp Worcestershire sauce

¼ tsp garlic powder

Sea salt & pepper to taste

Preheat oven to 375F. Line a large baking sheet with parchment paper. Set aside.

Drain and rinse chickpeas. Pat chickpeas with paper towels to dry and remove any loose skins (the drier the chickpeas are before cooking the crispy they will be after cooking).

In a large bowl toss chickpeas with oil, garlic powder, lemon zest and sea salt & pepper.

Arrange in a single layer on baking sheet and bake until crisp and light brown (approximately 45-50 mins) tossing halfway through cooking. Remove from oven and sprinkle with Parmesan cheese.

While chickpeas are roasting prepare dressing by combining all dressing ingredients in a medium bowl and thoroughly mixing. You may need to add a small amount of water to thin dressing to desired consistency. Refrigerate dressing until ready to serve.

De-stem the kale and tear or chop into bite size pieces. Place the kale, olive oil and lemon juice and a pinch of salt into a large mixing bowl. "Massage" the kale approximately 1 minute. This process helps to tenderize the kale. Set kale aside.

When ready to serve salad, combine kale, Romaine lettuce, Parmesan cheese and desired amount of dressing. Plate greens and top with crispy Parmesan chickpeas.

Sweet & Sour Red Braised Cabbage

Serves 4

½ large organic red cabbage, sliced ¼-inch thick

2 tablespoon grass-fed butter

2 tablespoons raw honey

¼ cup balsamic vinegar

Sea salt

Freshly ground black pepper

Sauté the cabbage:

Melt the butter in a large pot over medium heat. Add the thinly sliced red cabbage and toss to coat with the butter. Sauté until slightly wilted, about 5 minutes.

Add seasonings and simmer:

Sprinkle honey over the cabbage and toss to coat evenly. Add the balsamic vinegar to the pot. Bring to a simmer, then reduce the heat to medium low.

Cover and simmer until the cabbage is completely tender, stirring often, about 30 minutes total. Season to taste with sea salt and pepper.

Homemade Sauerkraut

6 Servings

1 head organic green cabbage, as fresh as possible

1 tablespoon Sea salt, or other colored salt

YOU'LL ALSO NEED

canning jars, wide-mouth quart size

canning lids (the metal disks with rings)

Chop or shred cabbage. Place in a large ceramic or glass bowl (don't use metal or plastic!) and sprinkle with salt. Stir with your hands or a wooden spoon until all the cabbage has been coated with the salt.

Let the mixture sit for about ½ hour. This allows the salt to pull the juices out of the cabbage.

After ½ hour or so (you can let it sit for hours), knead the cabbage with clean hands. Keep kneading until the juice begins to drip down to the bottom of the bowl (about 5 minutes). You might not get tons of juice, that's ok.

Pack the wilted cabbage down into your canning jars. Don't just dump it in the jars, really jam it in as well as you can. Make sure there's at least an inch between the top of the cabbage and the rim of the jar. Depending on the size of your cabbage, you should get about 2 ½ quarts of homemade sauerkraut.

Divide the cabbage juice from the bowl between the jars, then fill them with filtered water until the cabbage is covered.

Using one of the clean, outer leaves of the cabbage, press the cabbage below the surface of the water.

Screw your lid on tightly and set the jar in a dark place for at least three days to ferment.

Cabbage Stir fry

4 Servings

3 Tbsp avocado oil

½ medium organic yellow onion, sliced

1 head organic green cabbage, sliced

4 large cloves organic garlic, minced

1 Tbsp fresh organic ginger, peeled and grated

½ tsp ground cumin

3 Tbsp coconut aminos or gluten free soy sauce to taste

2 large organic carrots, grated

3 stalks organic green onion, chopped

Add the avocado oil to a large skillet with a deep lip and heat over medium-high. Add the onion and sauté, stirring occasionally, until onion has softened and begins to turn translucent. Stir in the chopped cabbage to the skillet – this will likely overflow the skillet at first. Stir as best you can, then cover. Cook until cabbage has wilted and begins cooking down, stirring occasionally, about 3 to 5 minutes.

Remove the cover and add the remaining ingredients, and stir well. Continue cooking until cabbage begins turning golden-brown around the edges and begins sticking to the skillet, about 5 to 8 minutes.

Parmesan Roasted Broccoli

Serves 4.

6 cups fresh organic broccoli florets

3 tablespoons extra virgin olive oil

3 cloves organic garlic minced

½ teaspoon sea salt

¼ teaspoon pepper

¼ cup Pork Panko

½ cup fresh grated Parmesan cheese

Preheat oven to 425F. Line a baking sheet with parchment paper.

In a large bowl add broccoli, olive oil, garlic, panko, and Parmesan cheese and mix until combined

our broccoli onto a baking sheet and sprinkle any leftover crumb mixture over
he top

ake on the top rack for 18-20 minutes

auliflower Mac & Cheese

Servings

½-3 lb head of organic cauliflower

tbsp extra virgin olive oil

tsp garlic powder

tsp black pepper

ea salt to taste

heese sauce:

tbsp grass-fed butter

tbsp cornstarch

¼ cup whole milk

oz sharp white cheddar cheese block

oz Monterrey Jack cheese block

tsp garlic powder

tsp black pepper

lt to taste

pping:

½ cups shredded Mozzarella cheese

eheat the oven to 375° and lightly grease an 8x8 baking dish. (You can also use a
ferent sized baking dish that's about 2 quarts in size.)

ash the head of cauliflower and cut off the florets. Chop florets into bite-size
eces and try to make them close to the same size.

Sauté cauliflower pieces with some olive oil, salt, pepper, and garlic powder over medium heat. Cook until it's partially softened but still have a little crunch in the middle. (This could take 10-15 minutes, depending on how large you cut the pieces.)

Take cauliflower out of the pan and set it aside.

Melt butter in the same pan and whisk in cornstarch. Keep whisking and slowly start pouring in milk. Keep gently whisking until all incorporated.

When the milk mixture is warmed, start adding cheese one handful at a time. Continue to whisk and add the cheese in handfuls until all is smooth and melted. Season with salt, garlic powder, and pepper.

When the cheese sauce is smooth, mix it with cauliflower and transfer into a greased baking dish.

Spread cauliflower evenly in the baking dish and top it off with shredded Mozzarella cheese.

Bake it for about 15 minutes. You can turn on the broiler until the top is golden but keep an eye on it.

~~~~~~~

Below is a week-long suggested meal plan for Long Term COVID-19 recovery. This is meant to be a guideline. All of the menu items are nutrient dense, caloric and high in protein. For long-term recovery, you will be eating like this for weeks at a minimum. I suggest you make a batch of every dish with extra servings that you can label and place in the freezer to save time.

LONG TERM RECOVERY SAMPLE ONE WEEK MEAL PLAN

	SUNDAY	MONDAY	TUESDAY	WED	THURSDAY	FRIDAY	SATURY
MEAL 1 BREAKFAST	2 SCRAMBLED EGGS IN GRASS-FED BUTTER, HALF SLICED AVOCADO, ½ CUP FULL FAT COTTAGE CHEESE W/BANANA	OVERNIGHT OATS (2 CUPS) APPLE CINNAMON; CUP OF MIXED BERRIES WITH GREEK YOGURT, LEMON GINGER TEA	BREAKFAST HASH BOWL WITH 2 EGGS, ORANGE SEGMENTS, LEMON GINGER TEA WITH HONEY	ALMOND FLOUR PANCAKES, GRASS-FED BUTTER AND APPLE CINNAMON COMPOTE, CHICKEN BREAKFAST SAUSAGE, LEMON	MUSHROOM ASPARAGUS AND GOAT CHEESE FRITTATA, BANANA SLICES WITH 2 TBL. NUT BUTTER LEMON GINGER TEA	OVERNIGHT OATS, STRAWBERY CHEESECAKE; 2 HARD BOILED EGGS; LEMON GINGER TEA WITH HONEY	WESTERN OMELET, ROASTED SWEET POTATOE SLICED AVOCADO LEMON GINGER T WITH HO

	S, LEMON GINGER TEA WITH HONEY	WITH HONEY		GINGER TEA WITH HONEY	WITH HONEY		
MEAL 2 SNACK	BONE BROTH (ANY KIND) 2 CUPS	KALE CAESAR WITH PARMESAN ROAST CHICKPEAS	BONE BROTH (ANY KIND) 2 CUPS	LEMONY LENTIL AND QUINOA SALAD	BONE BROTH (ANY KIND) 2 CUPS	3 BEAN SALAD	BONE BROTH (ANY KIND) 2 CUPS
MEAL 3 LUNCH	LEMON GARLIC PARMESAN CHICKEN WITH ROAST ASPARAGUS 2 CUPS	PINEAPPLE CHICKEN CURRY WITH CILANTRO COCONUT RICE	TOM KHA GAI SOUP WITH CHICKEN; SIDE GREEN SALAD WITH AVOCADO	LAMB BURGERS W/SPINACH AND FETA, SIDE OF ROASTED BRUSSELS	CHUNKY TUNA SALAD WITH GREEK YOGURT, TENDER LETTUCE, SLICED AVOCADO	PORK EGGROLL STIRFRY BOWL, CAULIFLOWER RICE	CHICKEN VEGETABLE SOUP, 2 CUPS
MEAL 4 SNACK	3 BEAN SALAD, 1 CUP LEMON GINGER TEA WITH HONEY	CAULIFLOWER MAC & CHEESE, 2 CUPS LEMON GINGER TEA WITH HONEY	BLUEBERRY CHEESECAKE SMOOTHIE LEMON GINGER TEA WITH HONEY	LEMON GARLIC HUMMUS WITH SLICED RAW VEGS LEMON GINGER TEA WITH HONEY	BANANA BERRY SMOOTHIE WITH YOGURT LEMON GINGER TEA WITH HONEY	LEMONY LENTIL AND QUINOA SALAD, LEMON GINGER TEA WITH HONEY	CREAM OF BROCCOLI SOUP, 2 CUPS, LEMON GINGER TEA WITH HONEY
MEAL 5 DINNER	ROPA VIEJA WITH BROWN RICE AND SAUTEED SPINACH	TROUT ALMONDINE WITH MASHED WHITE SWEET POTAOTES AND STRING BEANS	SALISBURY STEAK WITH MUSHROOM GRAVY, MASHED POTATOES, GARLIC KALE	SHRIMP PAD THAI WITH VEGGIE NOODLES	BEEF STEW, 2 CUPS	GARLIC CHICKEN AND BROCCOLI CASSEROLE, BROWN RICE	HERB CRUSTED PORK LOIN WITH BAKED APPLES AND ONIONS AND ROASTED SWEET POTATOES
MEAL 6 SNACK	LEMON GARLIC HUMMUS ½ CUP WITH PEELED SLICED CUCUMBER LEMON GINGER TEA WITH HONEY	BONE BROTH (ANY KIND) 2 CUPS LEMON GINGER TEA WITH HONEY	CHICKEN VEGETABLE SOUP, 2 CUPS LEMON GINGER TEA WITH HONEY	BONE BROTH (ANY KIND) 2 CUPS, LEMON GINGER TEA WITH HONEY	CAULIFLOWER MAC & CHEESE, LEMON GINGER TEA WITH HONEY	BONE BROTH (ANY KIND) 2 CUPS, LEMON GINGER TEA WITH HONEY	CREAM OF BROCCOLI SOUP, 2 CUPSS LEMON GINGER TEA WITH HONEY

Protein and Calorie Table for Key Foods on Your Recovery Diet

FOOD	APPROX. CALORIES PER OUNCE	APPROX. PROTEIN GRAMS PER OUNCE
CHICKEN MEAT (BONELESS SKINLESS)	60	5
LEAN BEEF	52	7
LEAN PORK	53	7
EGG, WHOLE LARGE	80	7
GARBANZO BEANS	34	3
KIDNEY BEANS	23	3
COTTAGE CHEESE WHOLE MILK	26	3
SALMON	51	7
HALIBUT	25	5
TURKEY MEAT	54	8
LAMB LEAN	57	7
SNAPPER	36	7
SHRIMP	20	4
NUT BUTTER	190	7
WHOLE OATS COOKED	17	1
GREEK YOGURT WHOLE MILK	28	3
GRASS-FED BUTTER	200	*
EXTRA VIRGIN OLIVE OIL	240	0
EXTRA VIRGIN COCONUT OIL	260	0
BROWN RICE COOKED	31	1
QUINOA COOKED	37	1.5
BONE BROTH CHICKEN	5	1
BONE BROTH BEEF	5	1.5
SWEET POTATO COOKED	25	.5
SUGAR FREE BACON COOKED (2 SLICES)	70	6

ALMOND FLOUR	170	6
ALMOND MILK UNSWEETENED (1 CUP)	30	1
COCONUT MILK WHOLE FAT UNSWEETENED (1 CUP)	45	0
WHOLE MILK (DAIRY) (1 CUP)	146	8
CHEDDAR CHEESE	110	7
AVOCADO	60	.5

*trace amount

I did not include every fruit and vegetable in this table because they are all relatively low in calories and protein. They are packed with nutritional value, however, and you should eat as much of them as possible with every meal.

n Conclusion

I'd like to wish you the very best on your journey back to good health. I sincerely hope that the recipes and ideas outlined in this book were helpful to you and your caregivers during this challenging time.

Made in the USA
Coppell, TX
23 December 2023

26810355R00057